CAMBRIDGE LIBRARY COLLECTION

Books of enduring scholarly value

Travel and Exploration

The history of travel writing dates back to the Bible, Caesar, the Vikings and the Crusaders, and its many themes include war, trade, science and recreation. Explorers from Columbus to Cook charted lands not previously visited by Western travellers, and were followed by merchants, missionaries, and colonists, who wrote accounts of their experiences. The development of steam power in the nineteenth century provided opportunities for increasing numbers of 'ordinary' people to travel further, more economically, and more safely, and resulted in great enthusiasm for travel writing among the reading public. Works included in this series range from first-hand descriptions of previously unrecorded places, to literary accounts of the strange habits of foreigners, to examples of the burgeoning numbers of guidebooks produced to satisfy the needs of a new kind of traveller - the tourist.

The Official Report of the Recent Arctic Expedition

In 1875, Sir George Strong Nares (1831–1915) set out for the Arctic in command of the ships *Alert* and *Discovery*, hoping to reach the North Pole and find the rumoured Open Polar Sea that surrounded it. The *Official Report*, published in 1876, recounts his fifteen-month journey in lively and often harrowing detail, describing freezing temperatures, frostbite and scurvy, vast, uncharted landscapes and treacherous, ice-choked waterways. It records the progress of the British Arctic Expedition with the scrupulous detail of a ship's log, providing valuable insights into the logistical complexities and human costs of polar exploration. 'We had arrived on the shore of the Arctic Ocean finding it exactly the opposite of an Open Polar Sea', Nares notes ruefully. A two-volume popular account of the voyage, published in 1878, is also reissued in this series.

T0364297

Cambridge University Press has long been a pioneer in the reissuing of out-of-print titles from its own backlist, producing digital reprints of books that are still sought after by scholars and students but could not be reprinted economically using traditional technology. The Cambridge Library Collection extends this activity to a wider range of books which are still of importance to researchers and professionals, either for the source material they contain, or as landmarks in the history of their academic discipline.

Drawing from the world-renowned collections in the Cambridge University Library, and guided by the advice of experts in each subject area, Cambridge University Press is using state-of-the-art scanning machines in its own Printing House to capture the content of each book selected for inclusion. The files are processed to give a consistently clear, crisp image, and the books finished to the high quality standard for which the Press is recognised around the world. The latest print-on-demand technology ensures that the books will remain available indefinitely, and that orders for single or multiple copies can quickly be supplied.

The Cambridge Library Collection brings back to life books of enduring scholarly value (including out-of-copyright works originally issued by other publishers) across a wide range of disciplines in the humanities and social sciences and in science and technology.

The Official Report of the Recent Arctic Expedition

GEORGE S. NARES

CAMBRIDGE
UNIVERSITY PRESS

CAMBRIDGE UNIVERSITY PRESS

Cambridge, New York, Melbourne, Madrid, Cape Town,
Singapore, São Paolo, Delhi, Tokyo, Mexico City

Published in the United States of America by Cambridge University Press, New York

www.cambridge.org
Information on this title: www.cambridge.org/9781108041539

© in this compilation Cambridge University Press 2012

This edition first published 1876
This digitally printed version 2012

ISBN 978-1-108-04153-9 Paperback

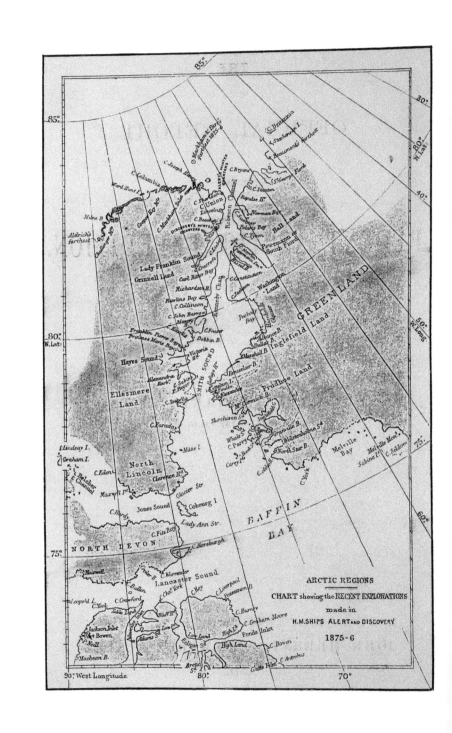

ARCTIC REGIONS

CHART showing the RECENT EXPLORATIONS

made in

H.M. SHIPS ALERT and DISCOVERY

1875-6

THE

OFFICIAL REPORT

OF THE

RECENT ARCTIC EXPEDITION.

By CAPTAIN NARES, R.N.,

COMMANDER OF THE EXPEDITION.

LONDON:

JOHN MURRAY, ALBEMARLE STREET.

1876.

ARCTIC EXPEDITION.

————◆◆◆————

H.M.S. "Alert," at Valentia,
27th October, 1876.

Sir,—I have the honour to report in detail the proceedings of the Expedition since leaving Upernivick on the 22nd
of July, 1875, as follows :—

Expedition leaves Upernivick.

The "Alert" and "Discovery," one ship in tow of the
other, left Upernivick, from which port I last had the honour
of addressing you, on the 22nd July, 1875.

A dense fog prevailing at sea I steamed to the northward
between the islands and the main land ; experiencing clear
and calm weather until arriving near Kangitok Island, when
the fog, stealing in from the sea, gradually obtained the
mastery, and completely enveloped us. The numerous
picturesque rocky islands and reefs in this sheltered laby-
rinthine passage are so incorrectly represented in the published charts that a pilot is at present a necessity. The one
who accompanied us, an Esquimaux, informed me that many
of the likely-looking channels are bridged across with sunken
reefs ; and from the many rocks we saw lying just awash
directly in our passage I have reason to believe his statement.

The large discharging Upernivick Glacier having only one
outlet, leading direct to the sea, its numerous icebergs of all
sizes are collected in great numbers by the eddy tides and
currents among the islets situated to the southward, and tend
to keep the channels completely closed until late in the
season ; but when once open in July by some of the bergs

B

grounding on rocks, and others, by their height above the flotation line, affording certain evidence of deep water, they assist rather than impede navigation during calm weather.

On the morning of the 23rd, after an anxious night, passed with a dense fog, and a strong tidal current, in a narrow channel, in which we could obtain no bottom with 100 fathoms of line at a cable's length of the shore, and with the "Discovery" in tow; during a momentary clearance of the atmosphere two Esquimaux in their kyacks were observed close to us. After consulting with them through Christian Petersen, Danish and Esquimaux interpreter, they volunteered to conduct us to an anchorage. On following them to the position they denoted, and obtaining no bottom with the hand-lead line at the main chains, I felt the bow of the ship glide slowly up on the ground. Through the fog we could then see that the land was within fifty yards of us. The Esquimaux had evidently not considered that our ships required a greater depth of water to float in than their own frail canoes. As it was nearly low water, and the tide still falling, I allowed the ship to remain quiet where she was; the "Discovery" still hanging to us by her towing hawser: and took advantage of the enforced delay by landing the ships' companies to wash their clothes.

The fog lifted slightly as the day advanced; and as the tide rose the ship floated without having incurred any strain or damage whatever. I then proceeded to sea; discharging the pilot, who was not to blame for our mishap, off the north shore of Kangitok, the outlying island of the group; after passing which the channel presents no difficulties.

Thinking that probably a distorted account of our getting on shore might reach Europe, at the last moment I wrote a hasty pencil letter to Captain Evans, Hydrographer, merely to point out how very unimportant the slight detention had been.

Crossing through the "Middle Ice," Baffin's Bay.

By 4 P.M. we had passed the Brown Islands, with a sea perfectly clear of ice before and around us.

Having given much study and consideration to the question; and a high and very steady barometer following a southeast wind, denoting that the calm settled weather we had lately enjoyed was likely to continue, I decided to force my way through the middle ice of Baffin's Bay instead of proceeding by the ordinary route round Melville Bay. Accordingly both ships proceeded at full speed to the westward, racing in company for Cape York, with only about a dozen icebergs in sight ahead, floating quietly on a calmly mirrored sea, to dispute our passage. As we passed out from the land the fog gradually dissolved and revealed a magnificent and unique panorama of the ice-capped mountains of Greenland, which give birth to the Upernivick Glacier, fronted by innumerable icebergs, and, at a long distance in advance, by the group of scattered black islets among which we had passed the previous night, and of which Kangitok is the northernmost.

Middle Pack.

At 1.30 A.M. of the 24th we ran into the pack at a distance of 70 miles from Kangitok. It consisted of open-sailing ice, from one to three feet, and occasionally four feet, in thickness. The floes were at first not larger than 250 yards in diameter, and very rotten, dividing readily, and opening a channel when accidentally struck by the ship. The reflection in the sky near the horizon denoted that while the ice was very open to the southward of us, it was apparently closer packed to the northward. About 6 A.M., when we had run 30 miles through the ice, it gradually became closer, and the floes larger, estimated as measuring one mile in diameter, and necessitated a discriminating choice to be made of the best channels. For 14 hours, during which time we ran 60 miles, the ice continued in much the same state, never close enough to suggest the probability of a barrier occurring, and yet keeping the look-out in the " Crow's Nest " fully employed. After 8 P.M. the channels of water became decidedly broader and more numerous, so I

gradually altered course to the northward, steering directly
for Cape York, the ice becoming more and more open as we
advanced.

At 9.30 A.M. of the 25th of July we sighted the high land
north of Cape York, and at 11 o'clock, much to the astonish-
ment of the Ice Quartermasters, who continually declared
"It will ne'er be credited in Peterhead," we were fairly in
the "north water," and able again to think about econo-
mising coal, having come through the middle ice in 34 hours
without a check: but it is my duty to add, with not a few
deep scratches along the water-line.

Middle Passage through Baffin's Bay.

In consequence of our having made a successful voyage
through the middle ice, it should not be too hastily concluded that a similar passage can always be commanded.
The middle pack is justly dreaded by the most experienced
ice navigators.

Large icebergs and surface-ice, floating in water at various
depths, when affected either by wind or an ocean current,
move at different rates; hence, when in motion, as one passes
the other, the lighter surface-ice, incapable of controlling its
course, is readily torn in pieces by the heavy massive iceberg; therefore, a ship once entrapped in pack ice among
icebergs, unless she has water space to allow her to move
out of the way, is constantly in danger of being carried
forcibly against a berg. On such occasions man is power-
less, for he can take no possible means to save his vessel.
Before steam vessels were used for ice navigation the masters
of sailing ships, being unable to take full advantage of a
favourable calm, very wisely seldom ventured to force their
way through the middle ice, and chose, in preference, the
chance of delay in making the safer passage through Melville Bay, where, by securing their vessel in dock in the
fixed land ice, they ran less danger of being nipped while
forcibly detained by the channels through the ice remaining
closed.

At the latter end of July with an open season, indicated by the main pack not being met with nearer than fifty miles from the land, in about latitude 73° 20′ and a continuous calm, to allow the northerly running current on the Greenland shore and the southerly running one on the western side of Baffin's Bay to open up the ice, I believe a passage can always be made by a steam vessel, but, unless this favourable combination of circumstances is met with, so far as the scanty knowledge we at present possess enables us to judge, the passage must still be said to be doubtful.

Soon after sighting land, and getting clear of the drift ice, the " Discovery " parted company to communicate with the natives at Cape York, while the " Alert " proceeded towards the Carey Islands.

Icebergs off Cape York.

A vast collection of icebergs, many of them aground, were thickly crowded together off the Cape ; and in lines parallel with the coast trending towards Conical Rock and Cape Atholl. In the offing they were less numerous : which I attribute to the southerly current, which we experienced the following day on our passage to the Carey Islands, catching up and carrying with it to the southward those that drift out from the main body to the westward beyond the influence of the north-running current on the Greenland coast.

Cape York Natives.

During the stay of the " Discovery " at Cape York, the natives were communicated with through Christian Petersen, Interpreter, and Hans the Esquimaux, but as the brother of the latter was absent on a hunting excursion for an uncertain period, Captain Stephenson wisely gave up the hope of obtaining his services for the benefit of the Expedition, and pushed on for the Carey Islands, where he joined company with the " Alert " ; the two ships arriving there at midnight of the 26th July.

Carey Islands, Depôt and Notice.

A depot of 3,600 rations and a boat were landed on the S.E. point of the S.E. island, and a record deposited in a conspicuous cairn on the summit. The "Expedition" then proceeded, steaming, with as much economy of coal as possible, northward through a calm sea, with bright clear weather. With the exception of the many scattered icebergs there was no ice in sight from the summit of the Carey Islands.

Passing between Hakluyt and Northumberland Islands, the ships were abeam of Cape Robertson by 8 P.M. of the 27th July. Ice apparently fast to the shore completely closed Inglefield Gulf east of Cape Acland but both entrances to the gulf were clear.

At 8 A.M. of the 28th July, five days and a half from leaving the anchorage of Upernivick, I had the satisfaction of seeing the "Expedition" at anchor near Port Foulke; with the entrance of Smith's Sound perfectly clear of ice and none coming to the southward with a fresh northerly wind.

"Polaris" Winter Quarters, 1872–73.

While Captain Stephenson explored the head of Foulke Fiord to ascertain its suitability as a station for winter quarters for any relief vessel coming to our assistance, Commander Markham and myself proceeded in a boat to Littleton Island and Lifeboat Cove, the scene of the wreck of the "Polaris." The cache mentioned by Dr. Emil Bessels and Mr. Bryant of the "United States North Pole Expedition" as the depository of certain instruments and boxes of books, was very readily discovered, but contained nothing. Articles of clothing and numerous small caches containing seal and walrus meat were scattered about the small peninsula in the neighbourhood of the late winter quarters; and near the ruins of the house, apart from each other, and without any protection, were found four or five boxes, each covered with heavy stones to prevent the winds moving them, and having the lids secured on by a rope. Besides one thermometer, unfortunately not a self-registering one, they contained scraps of skin clothing, old mitts, carpenter's tools, files, needles, and many small articles of the greatest use to the Esquimaux, but apparently they had not been disturbed since the abandonment of the station. A few books were found in the different boxes, and a copy of the log, or the actual log itself, from the departure of the vessel from the United States up to the 20th May the following year.

No pendulum, transit instrument, or chronometer was found. Three skin boats left on the shore, weighted down with stones, were in fair order. The smallest one was taken for conveyance to Cape Sabine.

Littleton Island Cairn.

On returning to the "Alert" we landed at Littleton Island and on the S.W. brow erected à cairn and deposited a notice containing a short account of the movements and prospects of the Expedition up to that time. There was no ice in sight from a high station on Littleton Island; but the sportsmen roaming over the higher grounds on the main land reported on their return that they had distinguished an "ice-blink" to the northward.

Port Foulke as a Winter Station.

Port Foulke is at present the best known station for winter quarters in the Arctic regions. A warm ocean current, combined with the prevailing northerly winds, acting at the narrow entrance of Smith's Sound, keeps the ice constantly breaking away during the winter, causes an early spring and a prolific seal and walrus fishery. The moisture and warmth imparted to the atmosphere by the uncovered water moderates the seasons to such an extent that the land is more richly vegetated, and therefore attracts to the neighbourhood and supports arctic life in greater abundance than other less favoured localities. In addition to this great advantage—of obtaining an ample supply of fresh meat—connected as its waters are with the "north water" off Cape

York, it can readily be communicated with every summer without more than the usual risks attending arctic navigation.

Cape Isabella.

On the morning of the 29th the two ships sailed across the strait for Cape Isabella, with fine weather; but as we approached the western shore a snow storm worked its way over the land from the interior, and reached us just as we arrived at the Cape. As the weather was so thick that no one on board the ships, except those employed in establishing the cairn and small depôt of provisions, could see its position, and there being therefore no reason for delaying the "Discovery," Captain Stephenson proceeded. The cairn was built on the summit of the outer easternmost spur of the Cape, at an elevation of about 700 feet from the water. On the boat returning on board at 5 P.M. I steamed to the northward for Cape Sabine; the wind having died away, but the weather continuing misty with snow.

First Ice sighted off Cape Sabine.

By 8 P.M., when we were 15 miles north of Cape Isabella, ice was sighted between us and the shore, and necessitated our keeping well out from the land.

Early in the morning of the 30th July, having run our distance for Cape Sabine I stopped steaming, and at 5 A.M. the mist clearing off, I observed the "Discovery" near the land apparently beset with a close pack five or six miles broad; no ice in sight to seaward. As I did not wish the two ships to separate, and the calm weather being favourable, I bored through the pack, which, although apparently close, opened sufficiently to admit of the slow progress of the ship until we gained the land in company with the "Discovery," and secured the ships in a convenient harbour, named after Lieutenant Payer, the successful and energetic traveller, two miles to the southward of Cape Sabine.

A depôt of 240 rations was established on the southernmost of the islets in a convenient position for travelling parties, a cairn being built on the summit of the highest and outer one, and a notice of our movements deposited there.

Pack off Cape Sabine.

The pack in the offing consisted of floes from 5 to 6 feet thick, with occasionally much older and heavier floes 10 to 12 feet thick intermixed with them, but all was very much decayed and honeycombed; still it could not be treated with the same impunity as the ice in the middle passage through Baffin's Bay.

Deceptive Impression on seeing " Open Water."

I may here draw attention to the deceptive impressions inexperienced people naturally receive when from a lofty look-out station they observe a sea unbordered by ice. The distance from Littleton Island to Cape Sabine is only 25 miles. On a clear evening, from an altitude of 700 feet, with the land and horizon distinctly visible, no ice was in sight from the first-named place, and the prospects of the Expedition as to attaining a higher latitude without trouble appeared to be precisely the same as when I looked over a boundless sea from the summit of one of the Carey Islands 100 miles to the southward, and yet the ships were twenty-four hours afterwards locked up by ice in a harbour near Cape Sabine.

From Littleton Island the inexperienced observer would conclude that there was an open Polar Sea ; from our present position he would as certainly conclude that his farther progress was for ever stayed, and that the sooner he looked for winter quarters the better.

The ships were detained at Payer Harbour for three days watching for an opening in the ice, getting under weigh whenever there appeared the slightest chance of proceeding onwards, but on each occasion, being unable to pass Cape Sabine, were forced to return. This resting-place proved to be an excellent station, well protected against the entrance of heavy floes, possessing a lofty look-out, and deep navigable channels to the north and south through which to proceed to sea immediately the ice opened with a favourable westerly wind.

Being advantageously situated near a prominent cape, where the tidal currents run with increased velocity, it is however subject to squally winds; but in icy seas during the summer, when awaiting the opening of the ice, they are rather an advantage than otherwise, striving, as they do with the sea currents, which is to be the chief worker in removing the impediments to a vessel's advance.

Advance up Hayes Sound—Princess Alexandra Haven.

Early on the morning of the 4th of August, after several hours of light south-westerly winds, the main pack, while remaining perfectly close and impenetrable to the northward, moved off from the land to a sufficient distance to enable the ships to pass to the westward round Cape Sabine. In the hope of finding a passage on the western side of the island, of which Capes Victoria and Albert are the prominent eastern points, sail was immediately made, and we succeeded, with only one short detention, in advancing twenty miles along the southern shore of Hayes Sound, and securing the ships in a snug harbour. In the neighbourhood the sports-men discovered a richly vegetated valley with numerous traces of musk-oxen and other game.

Two glaciers coming from nearly opposite directions, which instead of uniting in their downward course abut the one against the other, maintaining a constant warfare for the mastery, a never-ending grapple for victory, suggested the name of Twin Glacier Valley for the locality.

The ice in the sound was one season old and decaying so quickly that if not drifted away it would in a week's time present no impediment to the advance of a steam vessel.

Tides in Hayes Sound.

On the 5th of August the strong tides and a south-westerly wind opened a channel to the N.W., and we gained a few miles in advance; but, not wishing to expend much coal, were finally stopped in the light pack. After remaining sufficiently long to determine that the flood tide still came from the eastward, although the ebb or east running tide was apparently the stronger of the two, I pushed the ship through the pack towards the shore, and with Captain Stephenson ascended a hill 1,500 feet high. From this station, the appearance of the land giving no prospect of a channel to the northward, and, moreover, the westerly wind having set in in strength which we expected would open a passage to the eastward of Cape Albert, we decided to bear up and return to the entrance of the Sound; accordingly the ships made a quick run under sail to Cape Albert, arriving off which the wind died away leaving the ice loosely packed.

Beset in Pack.

A clear space of water being visible along the shore of the mainland to the northward, and the coast between Cape Victoria and Cape Albert affording no protection, I ran the two ships into the pack under steam, with the hope of forcing our way through, but before midnight they were hopelessly beset; and the floe, to which the ships were secured at a distance of 100 yards apart, drifting rapidly towards an iceberg. Both ships were at once prepared for a severe nip, the rudders and screws being unshipped. At first the "Discovery" was apparently in the most dangerous position, but the floe in which we were sealed up by wheeling round, while it relieved Captain Stephenson from any immediate apprehension, brought the "Alert" directly in the path of the advancing mass, which was steadily tearing its way through the intermediate surface ice. When only 100 yards distant the iceberg, by turning slightly, presented a broader front to the approaching ice, which then accumulated in advance of it to such an extent as to fill up the angle, and form, as it were, a point or bow of pressed up ice, sufficiently strong to itself divide and split up the floe, and act as a buffer in advance of the berg; and this it did in our case most successfully, our floe breaking up into numerous pieces. The ship herself escaped with a very light nip; and, sliding past the side without accident, was finally secured in the water space left in the wake of the iceberg by the faster drift of the surface ice.

The next twenty-four hours were spent in a constant struggle towards the shore through the pack, which fortunately consisted of ice seldom more than four feet in thickness, with occasional pieces up to twelve feet thick, formed by the over-riding and piling up of ordinary floes, which were afterwards cemented together by a winter's frost; the worn down rounded topped ice hummocks on these were from six to eight feet above the water-line. The icebergs, evidently derived from inferior glaciers, were from twenty to forty feet in height above water, and 100 yards in diameter.

Owing to the unsteady wind and the variable tidal currents we were unable to remain for long in any one pool of water—either the iceberg to which the ships were anchored turned round and carried us with it to the exposed side before we could change the position of the hawsers by which we were secured; or the pack ice, which was readily acted upon by the wind, drifting back the opposite way with any change, closed up the water space. Securing the ships in a dock in rotten ice in the presence of so many icebergs, was not advisable, and also would have carried the ships deeper into the pack to the southward. There was, therefore, no alternative before me but to get up full steam and dodge about as best we could, taking instant advantage of every change in our favour. The ships were seldom separated for long, and now as on all other occasions, they mutually assisted each other. The "Discovery" was handled by Captain Stephenson and her officers in the most masterly and daring manner combined with great judgment, qualities essential in arctic navigation. She, as well as the "Alert," ran not a few hairbreadth escapes. Once in particular when in following us through a closing channel between an iceberg and heavy floe-piece, before getting quite past the danger she was caught and nipped against the berg, and had it not been for a fortunate tongue of projecting ice would certainly have had all her boats on the exposed side ground away from her.   Fortunately, the moving ice pushed her clear, much in the same manner as it had done the "Alert" the previous day.

" Discovery " clearing a Nip

Having less beam than the "Alert," and a finer bow, with the very great advantage of an overhanging stem, the "Discovery" is better adapted for forcing her way through a pack.   It will be difficult ever to efface from my mind the determined manner in which, when the bluff-bowed leading ship had become imbedded in the ice, which by her impetus against it had accumulated round and sunk under her bows; and a great quantity, by floating to the surface again in her wake, had helplessly enclosed her abaft, the "Discovery" was handled, when advancing to our rescue; having backed some distance astern, for the double purpose of allowing the debris ice from a former blow to float away and for the vessel to attain distance sufficient for the accumulation of momentum with which to strike a second, coming ahead at her utmost speed she would force her way into the ice burying her bows in it as far aft as the foremast; the commanding officer on the bowsprit, carefully conning the ship to an inch, for had the ice not been struck fairly it would have caused her to cannon off it against ourselves with much havoc to the two.   From the moment of the first impact the inclination of the stem necessarily caused the ship's bow to rise three or four feet as she advanced from twelve to twenty feet into the solid floe and imbedded herself before the force of the blow was expended, as the ship's way was stopped, the overhanging weight, by settling down, crushed the ice down still further ahead.   Frequently on these occasions her jib-boom was within touching distance of the "Alert's" boats !   But after a little experience had been gained, such confidence had we in each other that there was not the slightest swerving in any one.

Steam Ships charging Ice.

Floes up to four feet in thickness, and in a soft state, that is melting not freezing, may be charged with advantage, thicker or harder ice had better be left alone.

It speaks well for our chronometers, and the manner in which they are secured, that their rates were little effected by the frequent concussions on this and on many after occasions.

By 8 A.M. on the morning of the 8th we had succeeded in reaching the land water off Cape Victoria, having sustained no more serious damage during this severe trial than sprung rudder heads, consequent on the frequent necessity of going full speed astern; all heartily glad to be out of the pack ice.

The two islands marked on the chart, on the authority of Dr. Hayes, as existing in the entrance of Hayes Sound are, as originally represented by the present Admiral Inglefield, in reality joined; the three capes named by the latter, north of Cape Sabine, are very prominent headlands and readily sighted from a ship's deck from any position north of Littleton Island. There is no sign of an inlet along the very slightly indented coast line between his Cape Camperdown and Cape Albert. His Princess Marie Bay is the inlet north of the land in the middle of the sound, but whether that be an island or a peninsula remains to be determined; and his Cape Victoria is evidently one of the headlands on the present Grinnell Land.

On altering Original Names on the Chart.

It is necessarily an unthankful office to find fault with our predecessors; but navigators cannot be too careful how they remove from the chart names given by the original discoverers, merely because during a gale of wind a bearing or an estimated distance is a trifle wrong; and when the corrector or improver is also himself considerably wrong, and in fact produces a more unreliable chart than the first one, he deserves blame. The names given to the headlands undoubtedly discovered by Admiral Inglefield should not have been altered by Drs. Kane and Hayes, each of whom published very misleading delineations of the same coast.

Hayes Sound.

It is as yet uncertain whether Hayes Sound is a channel or not. The flood tide coming from the eastward—the apparent continuity of the western hills and the absence of berg pieces or heavy ice high up the sound, would lead to the supposition that it was closed; but considering the general configuration of the neighbouring land and the fact that the ebb or east running tidal current was stronger than that during the flood (but this the westerly wind might have occasioned); and the numerous Esquimaux remains, which are usually found in channels, there seems no reason why we may not reasonably expect the existence of a narrow opening leading to a western sea. The very decayed state of the ice would be the natural result either from strong tidal currents in a long fiord or the increased strength of the ebb tide occasioned by an easterly set from the Polar Sea.

On passing what is called on the chart Cape Victoria, Commander Markham landed to ascertain the state of the ice, but a very thick fog and snowstorm coming on he was obliged to return. The ships were secured to the floe in Princess Marie opening which consisted of the last season's ice that had not cleared out: it was very much decayed but sufficiently strong to prevent our forcing our way through it—and in fact when pressing in with the flood tide it became so compact that at one time the ship was in danger of being driven on shore. At high water it opened and we succeeded in crossing the bay and securing the ships to the land ice in Franklin Pierce Bay on the southern shore of Grinnell Land.

On the morning of the 9th August, after depositing a record in a small cairn erected on a spur of the limestone hills, 200 feet above the sea, on the west side of the bay, one and a half miles east from Cape Harrison, we gained three miles of easting; but, being unable to round Cape Prescott, were compelled to make the ships fast to an extensive floe extending from that cape to Norman Lockyer Island, which stopped all further progress.

Walrus Shoal.

Franklin Pierce Bay, which is about three miles broad and two and a-half deep, and in which we found an unbroken smooth floe of one season's ice, is protected from any heavy pressure by Norman Lockyer Island and the Walrus Shoal, situated one mile further to the eastward; it is therefore a fit position for winter quarters. But, as far as we could judge during our short stay, there is very little game procurable in the neighbourhood.

The shoal was so named in consequence of the numerous ancient remains of Esquimaux found on the island, who, by the number of bones found lying about, had evidently subsisted principally on these animals. At present this neighbourhood may be considered as the northern limit of their migration, only a very few having been seen farther to the north.

Tidal Streams in Smith's Sound.

The comparatively sluggish tidal motion at the entrance of Franklin Pierce Bay denotes that the coast lies out of the main run of the stream, and if so, Princess Marie opening will probably prove to be merely a deep inlet.

In the extended basin of Smith's Sound the southerly current and the tidal streams run in a direct line between Cape Frazer and Cape Isabella, producing eddies and accumulating the ice in any open water space on either side of that course.

August being proverbially a calm month in the arctic seas, and the western mountains protecting the coast from winds blowing off the shore, the ice is inclined to hug the land, and, except during strong westerly winds, a large amount of patience must be exercised by any one striving to advance to the northward.

Pack in Smith's Sound.

The pack in the offing in the main channel consisted principally of old floes which did not clear out of the sound during the previous season, mixed with light one-season ice, formed in Kennedy Channel and its numerous bays, and in Hall's Basin. Amongst these were scattered numerous icebergs discharged from the Humboldt Glacier, and the few smaller ones on the eastern shores, and here and there a heavy blue-topped hummocky floe of ancient ice from the arctic basin of unknown thickness. By the scarcity of these the main drift of the northern ice is apparently in some other direction.

During the fortnight we were delayed in this neighbourhood, in the middle of August and the height of the arctic summer, a constant watch was kept on the pack, and as often as possible from high elevations, from which we were able to distinguish even the eastern shore, with its glacier and heavy barrier of fringing icebergs. Although small openings were seen occasionally, I am satisfied that north of Cape Sabine it was at no time navigable to the smallest extent, and that any vessel which endeavoured to force a passage through the middle ice here, where it is drifting steadily towards an ever-narrowing opening, as many have succeeded in doing in the more open sea of Baffin's Bay, would decidedly be beset in the pack and be carried with it to the southward.

We were delayed near Walrus Shoal for three days, unable to move more than a mile in any direction, until the 12th August, when, during a calm, the ice set off shore with the ebb tide, and allowed us without much trouble to steam past Cape Hawkes, and between it and Washington Irving (or Sphinx) Island—a very conspicuous landmark; but here the ice prevented any further movement, and the flood tide closing in blocked the channel by which we had advanced.

Cairns on Washington Irving Island.

A large depôt of 3600 rations of provisions was landed on

the northern side of Cape Schott, and a notice of our progress deposited in a cairn on the summit of Washington Irving Island. Two cairns were found there, but they contained no documents, and were much too old to have been built by Dr. Hayes in 1866, the only time any *known* traveller has journeyed past the position.

On the western shore of Dobbin Bay there is no shelter obtainable; and the tides run with much greater rapidity than off the coast farther to the westward.

During the next ebb tide, 13th August, after blasting a passage through a neck of ice, I succeeded in conducting the ships to the eastern shore, and docking them in an extensive floe four miles N.W. of Cape Hilgard.

Prince Imperial Island—Empress Eugénie Glacier.

A mile north of our position was an island, having a channel half a mile broad between it and the eastern shore of the bay, named Prince Imperial Island. The land ice which had not broken out this season extended from the island in a westerly direction across the bay. Several small icebergs were frozen in at the head of the bay, where there are some large discharging glaciers named after the Empress Eugénie.

The land, as far as our explorations went, was very bare of game, and not well vegetated. A floe of last season's ice was observed in the bay, between Cape Hilgard and Cape Louis Napoleon, but off each of those headlands the piled-up ice foot denoted very heavy recent pressure from the eastward.

On the evening of the 15th August, after considerable labour, we succeeded in blasting and clearing away a barrier which separated the ships from a water channel leading beyond Cape Louis Napoleon, but so narrow was the channel that, notwithstanding the extreme care of Captain Stephenson, the "Discovery" took the ground for a few minutes while steaming between the ice and the shallow shore.

By 8 A.M. on the 16th we had advanced to within five miles of Cape Frazer, but here we again met with a block. Calm

weather and spring tides caused much and constant movement in the ice, the main tendency being to drift to the
southward at the rate of about five miles a day.

Nature of the Pack.

The character of the pack had changed considerably, few
icebergs were seen that were not aground, and the floes consisted principally of old hummocky pieces pressed together,
of from twelve to twenty feet in thickness, the surface being
studded over with worn-down hummocks of a blue bottle-
glass colour, which denotes great age. In such ice it was
impossible to cut into dock on account of the time it would
occupy, even had we been provided with saws of sufficient
length. Our only possible safety lay in keeping close in
shore of grounded icebergs, but in doing so the two ships
were obliged to separate; the " Alert " securing to one,
and the " Discovery " forcing herself in between three
smaller ones farther in shore.

In Danger of a Nip.

On the two following days, during which the ice continued
to drift to the southward and westward, the constant movement of the heavy floes, nipping together with great force,
like the closing of a gigantic pair of shears, between which,
if once caught, the ships would have been instantaneously
crushed, caused much anxiety, and necessitated constant
watchfulness and much labour on the part of the officers and
crew; and all were much distressed at losing three or four
miles of the ground previously gained.

The rudders and screws were constantly being shipped
and unshipped, the midship boats were obliged to be turned
inboard, on account of the ice touching their keels, and
steam, when not in use, was always kept ready at twenty
minutes' notice. Beyond wrenching the rudder-head, no
serious damage occurred.

On the 19th, the highest spring tide, the ice near us
became more open; and from a high station on Mount Joy I

c 2

saw that we could at least regain our lost station and might
get farther north.

Cape Frazer.

Knowing that this was our last chance during the present
tides and until the strong westerly winds set in; and the
pack having opened for the first time, I risked boring my
way into the pack for two miles, and by so doing entered a
channel leading round Cape Frazer which had long been
considered as one of the most difficult milestones to pass on
our passage north.

By 9 P.M., after a few hours' delay during the flood tide,
which brought the ice inshore again, we were fairly in
Kennedy Channel, secured to a floe off Cape John Barrow;
only two days later in the year than when the "Resolute"
was blown out of winter quarters at Melville Island in 1853,
and with a fortnight of the navigable season still before us.

Between Scoresby Bay and Dobbin Bay there is no protection obtainable except inside grounded icebergs; none of
the shallow bays are deep enough to shelter a ship from the
pressure of heavy ice.

Error of Charts.

Soon after midnight the ice moving off shore, opened a
passage, and again allowed us to proceed; the water spaces
becoming more frequent and larger as we advanced northward. Passing the mouth of a large bay about ten miles
deep; after making a very tortuous course through the ice,
and many narrow escapes of being driven to the southward
again in the pack, we reached what we supposed to be Cape
Collinson, the second of two capes to the north of the large
bay, which must be intended to be represented on the chart
as Scoresby Bay. But as Cape Frazer is placed eight miles
and Scoresby Bay twenty miles too far north, and the rest of
the western land very incorrectly delineated on the charts,
it is difficult to say where we arrived, and yet for the present
it is necessary for me to describe the advance of the Expedition by reference to the published charts. I shall, therefore,

continue to do so with an occasional necessary reference to our correct latitude.

Between Cape Collinson and Cape McClintock, the north point of Scoresby Bay, is a slight indentation in the coast from half to three quarters of a mile in depth, but affording no protection. North of Cape Collinson the land trends slightly to the westward, and about three miles north of the cape turns sharp to the west forming Richardson Bay, which is much deeper than represented, probably four miles broad and six deep.

Ships stopped off Cape Collinson.

A heavy iceberg firmly aground two miles from the land in the shallow bay north of Cape Collinson, which had evidently never moved this season, prevented a compact floe from floating off shore. The same iceberg caught all the ice that streamed down the west coast and round Richardson Bay, guiding it out towards the S.E., away from Cape Collinson, off which, and between it and the iceberg, was navigable water. In this pool the two ships were secured, watching for an opportunity to get north, and during the forced delay employing our energies in trying, by blasting, to unlock the land ice from the berg, and let it drift south, with the hope of releasing the ice to the northward; but perhaps it is fortunate we did not succeed, as, by so doing, if the ice in the offing had not opened at the same time, our principal protection might have been lost, the iceberg itself being too small to form a pool under its lee sufficiently large for both ships, even if it had been for one.

A depôt of provisions was landed at Cape Collinson for our future travellers bound to the southward along the coast.

Current in Kennedy Channel.

The current was observed to run with greater rapidity to the southward than in the broader part of Smith's Sound. During each flood tide about five miles of ice drifted past us; for four hours of the ebb it remained stationary; thus about ten miles of ice drifted south daily, adding to the accumulation in the basin of Smith's Sound, unless, as is probable, it is carried as quickly into Baffin's Bay through the southern entrance.

On the north side of each point on this shore the ice had piled up a wall-like barrier from 20 to 30 feet high, but elsewhere there was not much display of pressure.

Attempt the Pack—Advance up Kennedy Channel.

On the morning of the 21st August, the water channels in the middle of the straits looking very inviting, we made a start at the top of high water, but were led by the ice so much out from the land, that I returned to our friendly protecting floe and iceberg until the next tide, first endeavouring to clear the nip of one against the other by ramming; but finding that it would cost too much in coal and shake of the ship to clear it completely, and too much powder to blast it away, I gave up the attempt. After consultation with Captain Stephenson, and considering that the constant open channels in the offing denoted more water farther off, the two ships started again at 9 P.M., just before low water, and, after a troublesome passage through about three miles of close heavy floe pieces, we passed into open leads of water extending to the N.E. up the straits. A bitter northerly wind, accompanied with mist and snow, freshening at the same time, carried the ice with great rapidity to the southward, and necessitated our beating to windward under steam and fore and aft sails, tacking frequently to avoid the heaviest streams of ice. After this snowstorm, the land remained covered with snow for the season.

By noon of the 22nd, after buffeting against the strong breeze, we succeeded in weathering the northern headland of the largest bay on the west coast, named on the latest charts Carl Ritter Bay, but agreeing by latitude and relative position with the neighbouring land with the north part of Richardson Bay. In this part of the channel there was very little ice, but three or four miles farther north a heavy pack extended across towards Crozier Island, and obliged us to proceed in that direction.

In the evening, the wind lulling, I took in the fore and aft sails, and steered through the most open channels to the northward, passing to the westward of Franklin Island, and at midnight we were abeam of Hans Island with perfectly clear water between us and the eastern land; but streams of ice prevented our approaching the western shore.

No deep inlet answering to the Carl Ritter Bay of the charts exists in its given latitude.

Stopped by Ice at Cape Morton.

Steaming to the northward I endeavoured to close the western shore south of Cape Cracroft, but the ice prevented our doing so, and forced me to bear up to the eastward for Cape Bryant. Passing which I found the pack extending across from Cape Morton and Joe Island to Cape Lieber, with a south-westerly wind constantly adding to it by driving more ice to the northward through Kennedy Channel. The "Discovery" then landed a depôt of 240 rations at Cape Morton for use of any travelling party exploring Petermann's Fiord, and the ships beat back to Bessels Bay; in the entrance of which we obtained a sheltered anchorage to the north of Hannah Island.

View of Robeson Channel.

On the 24th, the south-west wind still continuing, which I knew would open the ice on the western shore of Hall's Basin, I ascended Cape Morton. At an altitude of 2000 feet it was perfectly calm, with a clear sky. The prominent capes of the channel were clearly visible — Cape Union seventy miles distant, and Cape Sumner fifty miles, the one locking in beyond the other to within five degrees. All the west coast of Kennedy Channel, up to Cape Lieber and Lady Franklin Sound, was clear of ice; with navigable water through the ice streams in the middle of the channel far to the northward. From Joe Island to the north and east

to Polaris Bay the ice was closely packed, but between Cape
Lupton and Beechy was more open. Hurrying to the boat,
the ships were signalled to get under weigh, and we ran
quickly to the northward across the channel under sail.
Five miles north of Cape Lieber the pack obliged me to
enter Lady Franklin Sound, on the northern shore of which
an indentation in the land gave promise of protection. On
a nearer approach we discovered a large and well-protected
harbour inside an island immediately west of Cape Bellot,
against which the pack ice of the channel rested. Here the
ships were secured close to the shore on the morning of the
25th August.

Arrival at Discovery Harbour—Musk-oxen.

On entering the harbour we had the satisfaction of sighting a herd of nine musk-oxen, all of which were killed ; our
joy at the good luck of the sportsmen and ourselves being
greatly increased by the news that the vegetation was considerably richer than that of any part of the coast visited by
us north of Port Foulke, the Elysium of the Arctic regions.

Finding that the harbour was suitable in every way for
winter quarters, and the abundance of the spare arctic vegetation in the neighbourhood giving every promise of game
being procurable, I here decided to leave the "Discovery"
and to push forward with the "Alert" alone.

Low Temperature.

Owing to our high northern position, although the sun
was still above the horizon at midnight, its altitude at noon
was too low to affect the temperature much, consequently
after the 20th August the temperature of the air remained
steadily below freezing point for the winter, and the young
ice was forming at midday much earlier than it does in more
southern latitudes. Notwithstanding this, arctic navigation
depends so much upon the wind that I considered that the
transient arctic season of twenty days' duration was still at
its height. The ice in Robeson Channel was well broken up,

moving up and down the strait with the change of tide, and only waiting for a wind to open a passage along shore.

"Alert" and "Discovery" part Company.

Having strengthened my crew by embarking Lieutenant Wyatt Rawson and seven men belonging to the "Discovery," forming one travelling sledge party; on the morning of the 26th August the two ships forming the Expedition, the officers and crews of which had worked so harmoniously and successfully together, separated; those embarking in one, if the published charts and the statements of our predecessors proved correct, having the cheering feelings of in all human probability successfully completing the chief task assigned us; but the others, although elated at the prospects of their comrades and partaking generally in the inspiriting feelings, having a desperate fight to conquer the sensation of being left behind to play what they could not but consider a secondary part in the general programme.

On arriving at the entrance of the harbour the main pack was found to have closed in against the shore and completely filled up Lady Franklin Sound; some small floes streaming rapidly into Discovery Bay. In endeavouring to keep clear of these, the ship touched the ground at the top of high water and hung there for half an hour when, fortunately, by lowering the boats and lightening the ship a little, she floated again without damage. During the afternoon at low water the pack, which apparently uninfluenced by wind had been moving to the southward the whole day but fastest during the flood tide, drifted slightly off the land. Immediate advantage was taken of the welcome opening which enabled us to proceed north, but on reaching Point Murchison, the pack, extending completely across the strait, prevented all farther progress; there was therefore nothing for it but to return to "Discovery Harbour," where the ship was again secured at the entrance ready to advance at the first opportunity.

On the 27th we experienced very light N.E. winds. The ice in the channel continued to move to the southward, except during the height of the ebb tide, when it was either stationary or set slowly northward, but not sufficiently fast to open a navigable passage, although just before high water it appeared so ready to move that I was induced to recall the skating parties to the ship and keep the steam up.

On the 28th the ice was decidedly more open, and we were just about to move at 11 A.M. the commencement of the north running tide, when a thick fog enveloped us, and, hiding everything at more than twenty yards distance, effectually prevented our moving. Later in the afternoon it cleared off, but it was now low water, and on trying to move the ship I found that, although afloat, she was within a basin, surrounded on all sides by a raised embankment of mud, so, with the tantalizing prospect of an open channel before us, we were forced to remain until the rising water enabled the lightened ship to pass over the obstacle. Hoisting up the boats and signalling a final " good-bye " to the " Discovery," we succeeded in advancing to within a mile of Cape Beechy, fifteen miles N.E. of Discovery Bay when, in a tussle with a heavy floe-piece, the rudder head—which had been badly sprung some days before—became so injured that the rudder was nearly useless ; at the same time the pack was sighted pressing tight in against the cape on the northern side ; I therefore secured the ship inside some grounded ice and shifted the rudder.

While waiting at this part of the coast the sportsmen were fortunate enough to capture three more musk-oxen, a very welcome addition to our supply of fresh meat.

On the 29th the pack remained closed in to the northward of Cape Beechy until noon, when, at about the time of high water, from the summit of the cape, I observed it opening. The ship was immediately signalled to advance, and, picking up my boat on the way, we succeeded in reaching Lincoln Bay, but not without having to run an exciting and rather anxious neck-and-neck race with a heavy floe, which, setting in towards the beetling precipitous cliffs of Cape

Frederick VII., forming the south point of the bay, threatened to prevent our progress.

Lincoln Bay.

At the entrance of Lincoln Bay, which otherwise is much exposed, some very heavy floe bergs were aground on a bank, and they must to a great extent keep heavy ice from forcing its way into the bay during a south-easterly wind, in which direction the bay is perfectly open. The head of the bay, which appeared from a distance to be well vegetated, was filled with pack ice consisting of numerous small floe pieces less than a quarter of a mile in diameter intermixed with "rubble" or "boulder" ice, now all cemented so firmly together with this season's frost that we had great difficulty in clearing away a dock for the ship.

Depôt of Provisions landed.

On the 30th a depôt of provisions of 1,000 rations, for the use of travelling parties, was landed on the north shore of the bay. Soon after high water, the ice having opened out considerably, we proceeded to the northward; but in doing so, some large floe pieces of unusually heavy ice obliged me, much to my regret, to stand out some three miles from the land, thereby risking the ship being beset in the pack, which I was most anxious and careful to avoid happening.

Caught in the Pack.

On all occasions of viewing the ice in Robeson Channel, since it was first seen from Cape Morton, I had invariably noticed lanes of water stretching S.E. and N.W. across the channel from about Cape Lupton on the Greenland shore, to Cape Frederick VII. on the west side, due probably to this being the narrowest part or neck of the channel, and the ice jamming across the narrowing space north and south of it, according to the direction of pressure. Consequently, when at 3 P.M. the ice prevented any farther advance, observing many pools of water near us, and having two hours of the north-

running tide favoured by a light air still due, instead of returning to the safety of Lincoln Bay, I waited at the edge
of the pack, in the hope of its opening.   But in this I was
disappointed, for at 4 p.m., having just sufficient warning to
enable me to pick out the softest looking place near us, that
is, to get as far away as possible from the heavy ice, it completely encircled the ship; and she was hopelessly beset in a
very heavy pack, consisting of old floes of 80 feet in thickness, and from one to four miles in diameter, the intervals
between the floes being filled with broken-up ice of all sizes,
from the blue-ice rounded hummocks which were sufficiently
high above the water-line to lift the quarter boats bodily as
they passed underneath whilst grinding their way along the
ship's side, down to the smaller pieces which the previous
nipping together of the heavy floes had rounded and polished
like the boulders and pebbles in a rapid river.   Intermixed
with the pack, fortunately for us, was a vast collection of
soft pats of sludge-ice formed during the last snowfall : this,
if squeezed together before it is properly hardened into ice,
forms into plate-like masses with raised edges, each piece,
whenever moved, assisting to round its neighbour.

Increasing Thickness of Ice as we advanced North.

Since meeting the ice off Cape Sabine I had noticed a
gradual but considerable change taking place in the appearance and formation of the floes.   The heaviest that we first
encountered were not more than eight or ten feet in thickness.   Off Cape Frazer were a few more ancient pieces, estimated at the time as being twenty feet thick, but we now
know that that was far short of the correct measure.   But
up to the present time, when the main pack consisted
entirely of heavy ice, I had failed to realize that, instead of
approaching a region favoured with open water and a warm
climate, we were gradually nearing a sea where the ice was
of a totally different formation to what we had ever before
experienced, that few arctic navigators had met, and only
one battled with successfully; that in reality we must be

approaching the same sea which gives birth to the heavy ice met with off the coast of America by Collinson and McClure, and which the latter, in 1851, succeeded in navigating through in a sailing vessel for upwards of 100 miles, during his memorable and perilous passage along the N.W. coast of Banks Land from Cape Prince Alfred to the Bay of Mercy, but there sealed up his ship for ever; which Sir Edward Parry met with in the same channel in 1820 but, with the more difficult task before him of navigating against stream and prevailing wind, was forced to own conquered even him and his experienced companions; which, passing onwards to the eastward from Melville Strait down McClintock Channel, beset, and never afterwards released, the "Erebus" and "Terror" under Sir John Franklin and Captain Crozier; and which, intermixed with light Spitzbergen ice, is constantly streaming to the southward along the eastern shore of Greeland, and there destroyed the "Hansa" of the last German Arctic Expedition.

As our only hope of pushing north against the general set of the current, to say nothing of the extreme hazard of remaining in such a pack, consisted in regaining the shore, both boilers were lighted and full steam kept ready in order to take immediate advantage of any opportunity that might occur. During the night, at the top of high water, the pack, which previously had been drifting in a compact body to the southward, eased a little near the edge of the large and deep floating floes, in consequence of a difference in the speed of the surface and undercurrent; but before we were able to clear away a space of water at the stern sufficiently large to enable the rudder to be shipped the ice closed and obliged us to dismantle again. At the full height of the ebb current the pack again tried its best to open but with the same result.

Escape from the Pack.

Fully expecting a change at low water with much labour a working space was cleared under the stern but owing to the spare rudder being very badly balanced we nearly lost

our opportunity. At last, during a similar momentary
slacking of the ice pressure as occurred at the top of high
water, with a greater pressure of steam than had been
exerted even during the official steam trial, the ship commenced to move; when, by advancing and retreating, a
water space was gradually formed in which the ship could
gain momentum, and we pushed our way bodily into ice not
quite so close, and succeeded most providentially in reaching
the shore in Lincoln Bay.

Had we been delayed another five minutes the ship would
have been caught in the pack during the heavy gale which
set in from the S.W. the same evening and continued for
two days; and which, in fact, by forcing the pack to the
N.E., out of the Robeson Channel, enabled the ship to pass
Cape Union without any trouble.

Value of Steam Vessels in Ice Navigation.

During the late struggle, as well as on many previous
occasions, it was noticeable how futile the efforts of the crew
were to clear away the ice on the bow or quarter which im-
peded the movement of the ship compared to the enormous
power exerted by the ship when able to ram her way between
the pieces even at ordinary speed. Thus, steamers are enabled to penetrate through a broken-up pack which the old
voyagers, with their sailing vessels, necessarily deemed
impassable. At the same time there is a limit to the risks
which are advisable to be run; no ship has yet been built
which could withstand a real nip between two pieces of
heavy ice.

On the afternoon of the 31st August, shortly after the
ship was secured in her former position to the firm ice in
Lincoln Bay, the wind gradually freshened from the S.W.,
blowing slightly off the land, accompanied with a snowstorm and a threatening appearance of the weather.

So far as we could distinguish through the snow the main
pack was driven by the gale to the northward up Robeson
Channel but, knowing that it would take some hours to produce a navigable passage past Cape Union, I waited until

the morning of the 1st September when, with steam at hand ready if requisite, we passed up the straits, running before a strong gale 9½ knots an hour, between the western shore and the pack, which was driving quickly to the northward at about three miles' distance from the land.

Reach the Highest Latitude hitherto attained.

By noon, having carried Her Majesty's ship into latitude 82° 24′ N., a higher latitude than any vessel had ever before attained, the ensign was hoisted at the peak.

On hauling to the westward at the northern entrance of Robeson Channel we lost the wind under the lee of the land and were obliged to furl sails and proceed under steam ; at the same time the breadth of the navigable water channel was much contracted until off Cape Sheridan the ice was observed to be touching the shore.

Ice Wall.

In Robeson Channel proper, except where the cliffs rise precipitously from the sea and afford no ledge or step on which the ice can lodge, the shore line is fronted at a few paces distance by a nearly continuous ragged-topped ice wall from fifteen to thirty-five feet high. It is broken only opposite the larger ravines, where the soil carried down by the summer flood has, by accumulating, shallowed the water sufficiently to catch up the drifting ice as it passes, and form a line of more isolated ice hummocks. There the continuity of the ice wall is occasionally broken.

Floe-bergs.

But on leaving Robeson Channel, immediately the land trends to the westward the coast line loses its steep character and the heavy ice is stranded at a distance of 100 to 200 yards from the shore, forming a fringe of detached masses of ice from 20 feet to upwards of 60 feet in height above water ; lying aground in from eight to twelve fathoms water and, except where the coast is shallow, extending close in to the beach line. The average measurement of the ice in thickness as it floated is 80 feet; and it always breaks from the salt water floe of which it originally formed a part in pieces of slightly greater dimensions in horizontal measurements.

On finding the ice close in at Cape Sheridan, having made good 25 miles of northing since leaving Lincoln Bay in the morning, my only alternative was to secure the ship inside this protecting barrier of ice where she was accordingly placed during the afternoon; and a depôt of provisions of 2,000 rations established for the use of travelling parties.

The weather remained thick until the evening when I obtained a good view from a station about 300 feet above the sea level.

The coast line continued to the N.W. for about thirty miles, forming a large bay bounded by the United States' range of mountains—Mounts Marie and Julia and Cape Joseph Henry, named by the late Captain Hall, are so conspicuous that it was impossible to mistake their identity although more than thirty degrees out in bearing on the chart. No land was to be seen to the northward although, our wishes leading to the thought, we still hoped that the heavy clouds in that direction might hide it from our view; but considering the character and movement of the ice I was reluctantly forced to admit that it gave convincing proof that none existed within a reasonable distance and that we had arrived on the shore of the Arctic Ocean finding it exactly the opposite to an "Open Polar Sea."

Pack off Cape Sheridan.

The pack ice extended close in to Cape Sheridan and the shore to the westward of it; a pool of water being noticed on the east or lee side of each projecting point in the bay which the intervening ice effectually prevented our thinking of reaching. To the eastward the channel by which we had advanced was completely blocked by the return of the ice, and the ship, although fairly protected, was thoroughly embayed by the pack.

The last snow fall had covered the land completely to a depth of from six to twelve inches and the low sloping hills formed anything but a cheering landscape.

During the night the wind again freshened considerably from the S.W., and in a squall carried away the hawsers by which we were secured and obliged me to let go a bower anchor; this falling on gravel did not bring the ship up until she had drifted half a cable's length outside the barrier of "floe-bergs" from which the pack was slowly retreating towards the N.E. The gale continued all night and drove the pack two miles off shore; but its constant motion to the eastward kept it tight in against Point Sheridan and cut us off from all chance of advancing towards the north or westward.

I was much struck at the time by the pertinacity with which the pack kept its ground during this severe gale, and could not help fearing that there would be little chance of its opening out sufficiently to allow us to advance much farther this year; but knowing well the occasional inexplicable uncertainty in the movement of ice we still hoped for the best.

On the morning of the 2nd September the wind suddenly shifted from S.W. to N.W., bringing the pack rapidly in towards the land, and causing the ship to swing broadside on against the outer side of the heavy stranded ice; fortunately, the barometer having indicated the probability of a change occurring, steam had been kept ready and after a considerable amount of manœuvring the anchor was weighed. Our protected dock was so small, and the entrance to it so narrow and encumbered with ice, that it was with extreme difficulty, much labour, and no trifling expense in broken hawsers, that the ship was hauled in stern foremost; the united force of the wind and flood tide pressing at right angles to the course; it was a nice question whether the ice or the ship would be in first—and my anxiety was much relieved when, as the whole northern pack reached the outside of our friendly floe-bergs, I saw the ship's bow swing clear inside into safety : and the pack, instead of doing us an injury, considerably

strengthen our protecting outwork by forcing new pieces on
shore; at the same time we could not help foreseeing that
by so doing our chance of advancing when we wished was
proportionately lessened.

Formation of a Floe-berg.

The danger we had so narrowly escaped from was forcibly
represented to us all as the pack, with irresistible force,
swept past us to the eastward at the rate of a mile an hour,
and constantly added to the accumulated masses outside.

The projecting point of a heavy floe would first ground in
from ten to twelve fathoms of water; then the outer mass,
continuing its course, unable to stop its progress, would tear
itself away from its cast-off portion. The pressure, however,
still continuing the severed piece was forced, and frequently
by the parent mass itself, up the steeply inclined shore,
rising slowly and majestically out of the water ten or twelve
feet above its old line of flotation, and remaining usually
nearly upright. The motion was entirely different to that
produced when two ordinary floes some four or six feet thick
met together; then, the broken edges of the two pieces of
ice, each striving for the mastery, are readily upheaved and
continually fall over with a noisy crash. Here, the enormous
pressure raising pieces, frequently 30,000 tons in weight, in
comparative silence, displays itself with becoming solemnity
and grandeur. What occurs when two eighty-foot floes meet
we cannot say; but the result, as far as a ship is concerned,
floating as the ice does higher out of the water than herself,
would be much the same as the closing together of the two
sides of a dry dock on the confined vessel.

Ice in the Offing—Polar Sea.

For the next three days we experienced light westerly
winds; the ice remained close in to the coast, moving generally to the south-eastward but occasionally stopping and
closing up towards the N.W. during the ebb tide. During
the flood, pools of water, half a mile long by a quarter broad,

frequently formed on the south-east side of the larger floes, but they were always completely isolated from each other by several miles of heavy ice. Although a few large floes could be distinguished in the offing the pack within five miles of the land usually consisted of floes of less than a mile in diameter intermixed with a very large proportion of rubble ice, evidently broken off the large floes as they forced their way past the points of land to the N.W. of us; the whole forming as rough a road for sledge travelling as could well be imagined.

Sledge sent to explore the Coast to the N.W.

At this period, although all regular navigation was evidently at an end, I was naturally most anxious to move the ship from her exposed position before the setting in of winter; but the quickly advancing season warned me that no movement should be made without a reasonable probability of attaining a sheltered position. Accordingly, Commander Albert Hastings Markham and Lieutenant Pelham Aldrich started on the 5th of September to look at a bay seen from our hill station about eight miles distant from us to the westward. They reported that it was a well-sheltered harbour, thickly coated with this season's ice, but that the continuous wall formed by the grounded floe-bergs across the entrance to it would effectually prevent our entering.

After this report, with the temperature remaining steady between +20° and +10°, and the barrier of grounded ice which, although protecting, effectually imprisoned us, having increased in breadth to seaward for 200 yards; each heavy piece being compactly cemented in amongst its neighbours by the lighter broken up rubble ice which was carried in by the tidal current and frozen into position by the low temperature, I decided to commence landing such provisions and stores as were hampering the decks of the ship and which would not be required during the winter should we fortunately be able to move into safer quarters.

On the 6th, 7th, and 8th of September, we experienced a heavy fall of snow which, bearing down the young ice by its accumulated weight, allowed the water to percolate upwards and render the floe very wet and unfavourable for travelling on. But not expecting any decided movement of the ice during the neap tides, and having secured the ship with a bower anchor and cable to the shore, and landed an ample depôt for the support of any travelling party in the event of accident to the ship, which at the time did not appear improbable, Lieutenant Pelham Aldrich, accompanied by Captain Fielden, R.A., and Dr. Edward L. Moss, started on a pioneering journey towards the north, and Lieutenant Wyatt Rawson towards the south. The latter returned after two days' absence, having found the cape three miles from the ship—forming the entrance to Robeson Channel impassable by land on account of the steepness of the cliffs; and by sea in consequence of the continual movement of the broken pack, which prevented him venturing on it even with a boat.

Lieutenant Aldrich's party returned after an absence of four days. He had succeeded in establishing a depot of provisions, and exploring the coast line for a distance of twenty miles to the north-west. The travelling was found to be unusually heavy owing to the very rough state of the ice and the deep snow with its sticky wet foundation of sludge; indeed, so bad was it that although only laden with half weights, all three sledges broke down. The young ice in the few patches met with was too weak and treacherous to admit of heavy sledges journeying over it; one sledge broke through and was only recovered with much difficulty.

Water Channel round Cape Sheridan.

On the 10th September a westerly wind blowing off shore, force 4, combined with the ebb tide, opened for the first time since our arrival here a narrow channel, between the grounded ice and the pack which extended for half-a-mile beyond Cape Sheridan but trending out to seaward. On the 11th, the same wind continuing, the channel widened out until it was a mile broad and extended for six miles to the westward ending two miles distant from the shore. As this offered an opportunity of advancing a large depot of travelling provisions and boats by water, Commander Markham started with a strong party ; having first to launch the boats across the heavy barrier of ice inshore of which the ship was sealed up apparently frozen in for the season.

No Land to Northward.

The sky being fairly clear, this was the first day on which we were able to pronounce decidedly concerning the northern land reported to exist by the " Polaris." After a constant watch, and carefully noting the movement of the darkened patches, I was now with much reluctance forced to admit that no land existed to the northward for a very considerable distance. As seen through the light haze the dark reflection of the sky above the detached pools of water in the offing, in strong contrast by the side of the light reflected from the close ice, which in a great measure is similar to the bright glare reflected from a large sand flat, creates a very decided appearance of land when there is a mirage ; indeed sufficiently so as to deceive many of us when so anxiously expecting and hoping to see it. We therefore cease to wonder at the casual look-out men from the " Polaris " being mistaken ; but the more experienced on board should not have allowed themselves to be so readily misled.

During the 13th and 14th the wind from the S.W. gradually freshened until on the latter day it was blowing a very strong gale, force 10 in the squalls, and evidently extending over the whole extent of Kennedy Channel ; for the swell from the open water which it had produced on the weather shore extended round Cape Rawson, and reaching our position broke up all the light ice formed this season, driving it out to sea, the large grounded floe-bergs alone remaining, with clear passages between them, through which we could have readily passed if requisite ; but the main pack to the westward, although the channel leading to seaward had extended to between ten and twelve miles distance from us, still remained fast to the shore at a distance of about six miles from the ship.

Return of Depôt Party.

The ship was secured by a bower cable stern to the shore; one side resting against a large floe-berg and bumping slightly against it with the swell. During the evening it was blowing furiously with a blinding snow drift; and whilst I was thinking of the uncomfortable state of the travellers in the tents in such a gale I observed Commander Markham arrive abreast the ship. Although we were within 120 yards of the shore it was only by double manning the oars of the cutter that during an opportune lull I was able to establish a hauling line between the ship and the shore and so communicate with him; when it appeared that, having one man disabled from exhaustion, he had decided to push on for the ship to obtain assistance. With the help of the fresh men forming the cutter's crew Captain Markham and myself had the satisfaction of seeing the sledge party all on board before midnight and the frozen man's life saved; but the sledge crew, who had so gallantly faced the storm, were all much exhausted and in fact did not recover themselves for several days.

Water Channel to Westward—Unable to connect the Screw.

On the morning of the 15th the wind lulled considerably and the remainder of Commander Markham's party, under the command of Lieutenant Parr, returned; having passed anything but a pleasant time in their tents during the gale. On ascending our look-out hill I observed that the ice to the westward between the land and the channel in the pack had drifted to seaward leaving a clear road by which we could advance to a place of shelter. Making a signal to the ship, steam was immediately got ready and the rudder shipped but on lowering the screw we found it impossible to enter the shaft. While raising it again to clear away the ice a very thick snow storm came on with a blinding mist which, hiding everything from view, prevented our moving. Before midnight the storm was blowing as furiously as ever.

Closed in by the Ice for the Winter,

On the morning of the 16th, the gale still keeping the main pack clear of the shore; the weather cleared again and another attempt was made to ship the screw but without success on account of the accumulated ice. While endeavouring to clear it the wind gradually shifted round to the N.W., and we had the mortification of seeing the pack rapidly nearing the land. By 2 P.M. it had reached the shore-ice, and effectually closed us in for the winter. It never left the shore to the north-westward of our position afterwards; although a large space of clear water remained to the eastward between us and Robeson Channel so long as the wind lasted from the westward.

I may here add that on examining the cost line afterwards, both during the autumn and the following spring, I am firmly persuaded that our forced detention during the late gale was most providential. There was no bay on the coast open enough to receive the ship and the ice at the entrance of each was far too thick for us to cut or force our way through before the main pack had closed in.

Floe-berg Beach the best protected Position on the Coast.

Off the open coast where we were forced to pass our winter the heavy nature of the ice constituted our safety; grounding in twelve fathoms it was impossible that it could hurt the ship. At first I was rather anxious lest any lighter ice might be forced in, and that then the ship might be driven by it on shore; but as time advanced and nothing but ice of the same thick character made its appearance I became more reconciled to our position. It ultimately proved to be the best sheltered position on the coast from which a ready means of retreat was likely to be offered. In all other parts, the beach, either by being too steep allowed the heavy ice to force its way close up on to the shore; or, where shallower, left a sufficiently large space of water in which smaller and more dangerous ice-blocks were able to drift about before they grounded in about the same depth of water as that in which the ship floated.

During the following week preparations were made for the autumn sledging; each man being fully employed fitting his travelling clothing and preparing the equipment of the sledges.

Autumn Travellers start—Attain the Highest Latitude.

As soon as the shore ice was sufficiently strong Commander A. H. Markham, with Lieutenants A. A. C. Parr and W. H. May under his orders, started on the 25th September with three sledges to establish a depot of provisions as far in advance to the north-westward as possible. Lieutenant P. Aldrich left four days previously with two lightly equipped dog sledges to pioneer the road round Cape Joseph Henry for the larger party. He returned on board on the 5th October after an absence of thirteen days having, accompanied by Adam Ayles (P. O., 2nd Cl.), on the 27th September from the summit of a mountain 2000 feet high situated in latitude 82° 48′ north, somewhat further north than the most northern latitude attained by our gallant predecessor Sir Edward Parry in his celebrated boat journey towards the North Pole, discovered land extending to the north-westward for a distance of sixty miles to latitude 83° 7′, with lofty mountains in the interior to the southward. No land was sighted to the northward.

Return of the Travellers.

On the 14th October, two days after the sun had left us for its long winter's absence, Commander Markham's party returned after a journey of nineteen days; having, with very severe labour, succeeded in placing a depot of provisions in latitude 82° 44′ north, and of tracing the coast line nearly two miles further north, thus reaching the exact latitude attained by Sir Edward Parry.

Unable to communicate with "Discovery."

Being anxious to inform Captain Stephenson of our position, and the good prospects before his travelling parties in the following spring in exploring the north-west coast of Greenland, I dispatched Lieutenant Rawson to again attempt to open communication between the two vessels; although I had grave doubts of his succeeding. He was absent from the 2nd to the 12th of October; returning unsuccessful on the latter day having found his road again stopped by unsafe ice within a distance of nine miles of the ship. The broken masses of pressed up ice resting against the cliffs, in many places more than thirty feet high, and the accumulated deep snow drifts in the valleys, caused very laborious and slow travelling.

Autumn Sledging.

During these autumn sledging journeys, with the temperature ranging between 15 degrees above and 22 degrees below zero, the heavy labour, hardships, and discomforts inseparable from arctic travelling, caused by the wet soft snow, weak ice and water spaces which obliged the sledges to be dragged over the hills; combined with constant strong winds and misty weather, were if anything much greater than those usually experienced. Out of the northern party of twenty-one men and three officers, no less than seven men and one officer returned to the ship badly frost-bitten, three of these so severely as to render amputation necessary; the patients being confined to their beds for the greater part of the winter.

The sledges with their cargoes on four occasions broke through the ice, and individual men frequently; but these, becoming wet through, were made to change their clothing and so escaped any bad consequences. The frost-bites are to be attributed entirely to the wet sludgy state of some of the ice that had to be crossed. It so happened that heavy snow fell on twelve consecutive days forming a layer of lightly compressed snow at least two feet thick which in the snow drifts collected into ridges more than double that depth. The thin ice, not being sufficiently strong to support this additional weight, became borne down and allowed the water to ooze through; this being protected from the cold temperature of the air by its blanket-like covering, remained unfrozen, although the temperature was upwards of forty degrees below the freezing point; consequently whenever the travellers, inexperienced as they were at the time, were forced to drag their sledges over a road of this nature their feet became wet and afterwards frost-bitten a considerable time before they discovered it, when the tent was pitched in the evening, by which time the mischief had attained such an advanced stage as to defy all restoration of the circulation. The tent equipment became so saturated with frozen moisture that on arrival on board it weighed more than double what it did when dry before starting; and so anxious were all to escape another sleepless night in the stiffly frozen blanket bags, that on the last day a forced march was made by the northern party through the heavy snow to the ship in which the powers of endurance of all engaged were tried to the utmost.

All the travellers returned in wonderful spirits and full of pluck. Nothing could exceed the determined perseverance with which each obstacle to the advance of the party was overcome, or the cheerfulness with which each made light of the numerous unavoidable hardships they had undergone.

The sledges proved to be too rigid, the uprights breaking necessitated frequent stoppages for repairs; but by taking out the metal pins connecting them to the upper bearers, and depending upon the hide lashings, they afterwards stood the unusually heavy work admirably.

On no one day while the northern party were travelling this season could they have obtained snow of sufficient consistency to enable them to build snow houses for shelter by night. Lieutenant Rawson, finding harder snow in the southern ravines, was able to construct a snow house on one occasion.

The advantageous results of the autumn travelling, in

addition to the advance of provisions for future use, were, first, a considerable gain in experience in arctic sledging; and secondly, by our greater good fortune in finding continuous land over or near which to travel, we succeeded in wresting from Sir Edward Parry and his companions their gallantly achieved distinction of having advanced the British Flag to the highest northern latitude. I have grouped the names of himself and his followers together on the chart in the latitude to which they attained in 1827.

Preparations for the Winter.

On the return of the travelling parties, the sun having bidden us farewell, preparations were made for the winter; the ship was housed over, all the provisions and stores which could withstand the weather, and for which room could not be found below hatches, were deposited on shore, and the habitable deck cleared as much as possible.

By carefully covering over the engine-room hatches with a thick layer of snow the cold, throughout the winter, was kept from penetrating downwards into the lower part of the ship. The temperature of the holds and engine-room, without the use of fires, always remaining above + 28·5, the temperature of the surrounding water; and the fire-pumps which had their suction pipes more than six feet below the water-line remained serviceable to the last.

Arctic Winter.

The long arctic winter with its unparalleled intensity and duration of darkness produced by an absence of sunlight for 142 days, was passed by each individual on board with much cheerfulness and contentment. Owing to the sameness in the daily routine, which, when looking into futurity, is thought to entail a long duration of dreary monotony, the time, in reality, passed with great rapidity; and in January, when the first glimmering increase in the mid-day twilight began to lengthen sensibly day by day, the want of light was scarcely noticed by any one; and not until the sun actually returned on the 1st of March did we in any way realize the intense darkness we must have experienced for so long a period.

The manifold ordinary duties of the ship—to which were added the constant repair of the snow embankment which, in consequence of our being frozen in close to a stranded piece of ice, was thrown down every spring tide—kept the ship's company fully employed, and gave them plenty of exercise during the day.

On five evenings in the week a school, formed on the lower deck under Commander Markham and several of the officers, was well attended; each Thursday being devoted to lectures, songs in character, and readings, with occasional theatrical representations; the whole so admirably arranged and conducted by Commander Markham as to keep up the pleased interest of all for the whole period.

The ventilation of the ship received the unceasing attention of Dr. Thomas Colan and myself; and owing to the large extra space amidships, left little or nothing to be desired in that respect.

The health of the officers and crew, with only one exception, was most excellent; and the habitable deck as dry as is possible in these regions in a ship without an extraordinary expenditure of coal.

Preparations for Spring travelling.

With the arrival of the new year preparations for the spring travelling campaign commenced; the dogs being exercised daily under the superintendence of Mr. George Le Clere Egerton, Sub-Lieutenant, as soon as there was sufficient light.

Movement of the Ice.

The pack in the offing remained in motion until the first week in November, when it gradually settled itself into position for the winter; the last pool of water being seen on the 16th of the month off Cape Rawson at the entrance to Robeson Channel.

No movement whatever occurred in the ice during the winter; except the formation of a tidal crack outside the grounded ice which opened two or three feet during the spring tides.

Winds and Weather.

Although we had frequent evidence of strong winds prevailing in Robeson Channel the weather at our winter quarters was remarkably calm ; indeed we may be said to have wintered on the border of a Pacific Sea. The prevailing wind was from the westward ; we never experienced any easterly winds ; it always blew off the land. Had it not been for the intervening calms, the persistent westerly winds might have been well called a trade wind. On only two days were we prevented by the wind and accompanying snowdrift from taking exercise outside the ship.

This quiet state of the atmosphere was productive of the severest cold ever experienced in the arctic regions.

Temperature.

Early in March during a long continuance of cold weather,—

The "Alert" registered a minimum of 73·7 below zero.

The "Discovery" at the same time 70·5.

In 1850 the "North Star," at Wolseholme Sound, in latitude 76° 30′ N., recorded 69·5 below zero.

The "Alert's" minimum temperature for twenty-four hours was 70·31 below zero.

The "Discovery's" minimum temperature for twenty-four hours was 67·0 below zero.

Dr. Kane's at Rensselaer Harbour, in latitude 78° 37′ N. in 1854, 58·01 below zero.

Previously the longest continuance of cold weather recorded, that by Sir Edward Belcher at Northumberland Sound, in latitude 76° 52′ N., in 1853, was a mean temperature for ten consecutive days of 48·9 below zero.

The "Discovery" experienced a mean temperature for seven consecutive days of 58·17 ditto.

The " Alert " experienced a mean temperature for thirteen days of 58·9 ditto;

And for five days and nine hours of 66·29.

During February mercury remained frozen for fifteen consecutive days; a south-westerly gale, lasting four days, then brought warmer weather; immediately the wind fell cold weather returned and the mercury remained frozen for a further period of fifteen days.

Snow fall.

After the heavy snow fall in the autumn previously alluded to very little fell; and much trouble was experienced in obtaining sufficient for embanking the ship it being necessary to drag some from the shore for that purpose. Owing to the small quantity which fell during the winter, estimated at from six to eight inches, the summits of the coast hills were uncovered by the wind and remained so until May and the early part of June, when we again experienced a heavy snow fall, estimated at a mean thickness of one foot.

In the valleys and on the shores having an eastern aspect the snow which fell remained light and, unless snow shoes were used, caused very heavy travelling. In the unprotected valleys and on the weather coasts the snow was sufficiently compact to afford fair travelling; much the same as that experienced in southern latitudes where the more variable winds harden the snow everywhere.

Aurora.

Light flashes of aurora were occasionally seen on various bearings; but most commonly passing through the zenith. None were of sufficient brilliancy to call for notice. The phenomena may be said to have been insignificant in the extreme and, as far as we could discover, were totally unconnected with any magnetic or electric disturbance.

Magnetic Observations.

During the winter Commander Albert H. Markham and Lieutenant George A. Giffard employed themselves with much diligence and perseverance at the magnetic observatory, situated on shore in a series of large and lofty snow houses which were connected together with a covered snow gallery.

Weekly observations were made with Barrows' dip circle for determining the inclination; and by means of Lloyd's needles for the total (relative) force. Occasionally these observations were repeated on the same day.

The absolute horizontal intensity was obtained once every three weeks, and a series of hourly differential observations were obtained with the portable declination magnetometer on several consecutive days in the months of December, January, and February.

At various places between Disco and the "Alert's" winter quarters, whenever opportunities offered, observations for inclination and total force were taken with Mr. Fox's instrument; observations for determining the absolute declination were also taken when opportunities occurred.

Lieutenant Pelham Aldrich superintended the meteorological observations, also observations with Sir C. Wheatstone's polariscope; and Lieutenant Alfred A. C. Parr, notwithstanding the severe season, obtained a good series of astronomical observations; also observations with the spectroscope and Sir William Thomson's portable electrometer.

I have not hitherto alluded to the services of Captain Fielden, Paymaster, R.A., Naturalist to the Expedition; preferring that the report on the numerous scientific subjects to which he has directed his attention should emanate from himself: I will merely state here that no one moment has been lost by this indefatigable collector and observer. He has, moreover, by his genial disposition and ready help on all occasions, won the friendship of all, and I feel confident that their Lordships will highly appreciate his valuable services. I am only doing him justice when I state that he has been to this Expedition, what Sabine was to that under the command of Sir Edward Parry.

Dr. Edward Moss, a highly skilled and talented observer, in addition to his medical duties, kept himself fully employed in many branches of natural science; his investigations embraced studies of the floe-bergs and floes, principally chlorine estimations, specific gravity estimations by Buchanon's method, and microscopy of dust strata.

The chlorine and specific gravity estimations, and the microscopy of winter sea water. Examination of air precipitates. Estimation of carbonic acid and watery vapour in air. Some experiments on the brittleness of iron at low temperatures.

Game procured.

The vicinity of our winter quarters proved to be unfavoured by game. On our first arrival, a few ducks were seen and five shot; and during the winter and spring three hares were shot in the neighbourhood of the ship. This completes our list up to the end of May.

In March, a wolf suddenly made his appearance; and the same day the track of three musk-oxen or reindeer were seen within two miles of the ship, but they had evidently only paid us a flying visit.

In July six musk-oxen were shot the only ones seen in our neighbourhood.

The travelling parties were only slightly more fortunate in obtaining game.

In June, a few ptarmigan, ducks and geese were shot and used by the sick. In July and August they obtained a ration of fresh meat daily.

In March and the beginning of April about two dozen ptarmigan passed the ship flying towards the N.W. in pairs: finding no vegetation uncovered by snow in our neighbourhood, they flew on seeking better feeding grounds, and were nearly all shot subsequently by the outlying parties near Cape Joseph Henry. In the middle of May snow-buntings and knots arrived. A number of the young of the latter were killed in July, but no nests or eggs were found. Early in June ducks and geese passed in small flocks of about a dozen, flying towards the N.W., but, owing to a heavy fall of snow, lasting three days, which covered the land more completely than at any other time during our stay, at least half the number returned to the southward not pleased with their prospects so far north.

Two dozen small trout were caught during the autumn and summer in lakes from which they could not possibly escape to the sea.

The total game list for the neighbourhood of the " Alert's " winter quarters is as follow :—

	Musk-oxen.	Hares.	Geese.	King Ducks.	Eider Ducks.	Long-tailed Ducks.	Ptarmigan.	Walrus.	Seals.	Foxes.
In winter quarters	6	7	67	12	..	9	..	..	1	3
By short service sledging parties	..	13	3	5	..	..	10	..	..	..
Total . . .	6	20	70	17	..	9	10	..	1	3

On the 1st March the sun returned after its long absence.

The sledging season being now near at hand, I prepared orders for Captain Stephenson to employ the whole force at his disposal in exploration of the neighbouring shore and the north coast of Greenland instead of sending a party to communicate with Smith's Sound; as I considered that a sledge-party employed on that duty this season would be performing unnecessary work; and that in the event of their Lordships communicating with Littleton Island, and finding that I had not visited it, they would understand that the Expedition was well placed for exploration far north, and that all was going on satisfactorily.

Dog-sledge starts to communicate with H.M.S. " Discovery."

The 4th of March was the day fixed for the dog-sledge to start to open communication with the " Discovery," should

E

the weather be favourable; but the severe cold which we then experienced prevented their starting. The temperature remained unusually low until the 12th, when it rose to minus 35°, and the weather being fine and settled, Mr. George Le Clere Egerton, Sub-Lieutenant, started in charge of the dog-sledge, accompanied by Lieutenant Wyatt Rawson, belonging to the "Discovery," whom I wished to consult with Captain Stephenson concerning the exploration of the Greenland coast, and Christian Petersen, Interpreter. As I knew that this journey was sure to entail very severe labour, Frederick, the Esquimaux dog-driver, not being a strong man, was left on board. Four days afterwards, the temperature having risen considerably in the interval with a strong wind from the southward, the party returned in consequence of the severe illness of Petersen. He was taken ill on the second march with cramp in the stomach; and afterwards nothing could keep him warm. The tent being very cold, the two officers burrowed out a snow hut and succeeded in raising the temperature inside to plus 7°; but the patient still remained in an unsatisfactory condition: and it was only by depriving themselves of all their own warm clothing and at the expense of the heat of their own bodies that they succeeded, after great persistence, in restoring the circulation in his extremities to some extent. The following day, Petersen being no better, they wisely determined to return with him immediately to the ship. During this journey of sixteen miles both Mr. Egerton and Lieutenant Rawson behaved most heroically; and, although frequently very seriously frost-bitten themselves, succeeded in keeping life in the invalid until they arrived on board. He was badly frost-bitten in the feet, both of which had subsequently to be amputated. Notwithstanding the professional ability and incessant watchful care of Dr. Thomas Colan, he never recovered from the severe shock his system had received on this occasion, and eventually expired from exhaustion three months afterwards.

He leaves a wife and family, living in Copenhagen, who, I trust, will receive a pension.

Second Start of Dog-sledge to communicate with " Discovery."

On the 20th March, with fine weather and a temperature of 30° below zero, Mr. Egerton and Lieutenant Rawson, having partially recovered from their most praiseworthy exertions when attending Petersen, again started for the " Discovery," accompanied by two seamen ; where they succeeded in reaching on the sixth day after a hard scramble over the rough ice in Robeson Channel and along the steep snow slopes formed at the foot of the precipitous coast cliffs. No water was met with beyond that formed in the tidal crack close to the shore. The temperature throughout the journey ranged from minus 42° to minus 24°.

Preparations for Spring Sledging.

During the latter part of March the sledge crews were fully employed preparing their provisions and equipping the sledges for the spring journeys. Long walks were taken for exercise ; and a depot of provisions was placed a few miles to the southward for the use of the Greenland Division.

On the 3rd April the seven sledges and crews, numbering fifty-three officers and men, started on their journeys with as bright prospects before them as any former Arctic travellers ;—everyone in apparently the best possible health and, while knowing the severe labour and hardships they would have to undergo, all cheerful, and determined to do their utmost. A finer body of picked men than the crews of the three extended sledge parties were never previously collected together.

Commander Albert H. Markham, seconded by Lieutenant Alfred A. C. Parr, with two boats equipped for an absence of seventy days, was to force his way to the northward over the ice ; starting off from the land near Cape Joseph Henry.

Three sledge crews, under the respective commands of Dr. Edward Moss, who in addition to his duties as Medical Officer to the division volunteered to assume executive charge, and Mr. George White, Engineer, also a volunteer; accompanying them as far as their provisions would allow. Lieutenant Pelham Aldrich, assisted by a sledge crew under

the command of Lieutenant George A. Giffard, was to explore
the shores of Grant Land towards the north and west along
the coast line he had discovered during the previous autumn.

Difficulties foreseen in the Northern Route.

In regard to the first of these two journeys, that under-
taken over the ice towards the north, it is my duty to its
Commander and his followers to state that, knowing the
extremely rough road over which they would be obliged to
travel, I had little hope that they would reach a high latitude, for their daily progress with light or heavy sledges
must necessarily be very slow. I thought it best, nevertheless, to make the experiment, to prove whether or not the
Pole could be reached by a direct course over the ice without continuous land along which to travel. Having such
willing and determined leaders as Commander Markham and
Lieutenant Parr, and the pick of the ship's company, who
themselves were all chosen men out of numbers at hand, I
sent them forth with full confidence that whatever was
possible they would perform.

In organizing this party, nothing was known of the
movements of the Polar ice. I was even in doubt whether
it was not always in motion in the offing, consequently I
decided that boats must be carried of sufficient capacity for
navigation, and not merely for ferrying purposes. This
necessitated very heavy weights being dragged. It was
also necessary that the party should carry a heavy load of
provisions, for, owing to our clear weather and lofty look-out
station, we had previously ascertained that no land existed
within a distance of fifty miles of Cape Joseph Henry.

When a sledge party have to drag a boat, even with only
a few days' provisions and over a smooth floe, double trips
are necessary over the same road daily, in the same manner
as Sir Edward Parry was compelled to journey in 1827;
consequently, the utmost limit that could be transported in
this way with two trips on level ice was chosen, and this
provided the party for an absence from the land for sixty-
three days. The plan usually resorted to of reducing the

weights carried by the advance party by providing a chain of supporting sledges is not applicable when each assisting sledge requires a boat capable of carrying its crew.

Return of Dog-sledge from " Discovery."

On the day following the departure of our travelling parties, Mr. Egerton and Lieutenant Rawson returned from the " Discovery " after a rough journey, with a temperature ranging between 44° and 15° below zero, but all in good health and spirits ; and, beyond sore noses and tips of fingers from frost-bites, none the worse for their cold journey.

The news from the " Discovery " was most cheering, with the exception that, although they had succeeded in obtaining upwards of thirty musk-oxen, one man was in the sick list with a bad attack of scurvy. With this exception the crew of the " Discovery " had passed a very comfortable winter. Plenty of cheerful work leading to and inducing constant employment of mind and body coupled with a fair share of mirthful relaxation and a frequent meal of fresh meat. I refer you, Sir, to Captain Stephenson's full report for a detail of his proceedings. His crew were preparing for the exploration of Lady Franklin Sound and the coast of Greenland.

Return of First Auxiliary Sledge.

On the 8th April the first supporting sledge returned from Commander Markham's and Lieutenant Aldrich's parties. As usual on the first starting, several of the travellers were much distressed by the severe and unaccustomed work and the cold weather preventing sleep at night, but were gradually improving. One man, who had been ailing slightly during the last month, was sent back, and one of the crew of the supporting sledge returned with a frost-bite, the only serious case during the season; although the travellers, on two days out of the six that this party were away, experienced a temperature of minus 46 degrees.

On the 10th April, Lieutenant Wyatt Rawson and Sub-Lieutenant George Le Clere Egerton, having somewhat re-

covered after their cold journey to the " Discovery," equipped
with light sledges started to ascertain the nature of the ice
in Robeson Channel and to mark a convenient road across it
for the heavier exploring sledges coming north from the
"Discovery" under the command of Lieutenant Lewis A.
Beaumont.

On the 14th of April the second division of the supporting
sledges returned reporting the main parties to have settled
steadily down to their work; and, with the exception of one
marine suffering from debility who was sent back, all were
in good health and capital spirits. The temperature had
fortunately risen to about minus 26 degrees. The very cold
weather had tried the party much, and there had been
numerous light cases of frost-bites which, but for the presence and care of Dr. Moss, might have proved serious. The
appearance of the ice within six miles of the land was anything but cheering to the northern party; but they looked
forward with hope that the floes would get larger and less
broken up as they advanced.

Ration of Tea preferred to Rum.

Each sledge carried extra tea in lieu of the usual mid-day
allowance of spirits. Both men and officers were unanimous
in favour of the change and willingly put up with the misery
of standing still in the cold with cold feet during the long
halt needed for the purpose of boiling the water; and all
agreed that they worked better after the tea lunch than
during the forenoon.

Greenland Division of Sledges arrive from H.M.S. " Dis-covery."

On the 16th, Lieutenant Lewis A. Beaumont and Dr.
Richard W. Coppinger arrived from the " Discovery," having
been ten days performing a travelling distance of 76 miles
with light sledges, so broken up and difficult was the nature
of the ice in Robeson Channel. They brought news that the
ice was continuous and afforded fair travelling across Hall's

Basin and that the depot of provisions at Polaris Bay was in good condition and fit for use. These circumstances enabled me to arrange for Lieutenant Beaumont to proceed with lightly laden sledges along the Greenland coast to the eastward; and after completing his journey, to fall back on the "Polaris" depot before the 15th June; by which time two boats would be carried across the straits from the "Discovery," ready for his retreat should the ice have broken up.

On the 18th, Lieutenant Rawson and Mr. Egerton returned, having succeeded in crossing the channel without finding more than the usual difficulties amongst the heavy hummocks; which they had now become so accustomed to. They had landed on the Greenland coast north of the position marked as Repulse Harbour; which proves to be only a slight indentation in the coast line, having a fresh water lake inshore of it, which from an inland view might readily be mistaken for a harbour.

On the 20th of April Lieutenant Beaumont, accompanied by Lieutenant Rawson and Dr. Coppinger, started for his Greenland exploration; the few days' rest having materially benefited his men, who may be said to have started from the "Discovery" inexperienced in Arctic sledging; that ship having had no autumn travelling in consequence of the ice remaining in motion until a very late period of the season.

On the 23rd of April Captain Stephenson and Mr. Thomas Mitchell, Assistant Paymaster in charge, arrived from the "Discovery," and I had the advantage of consulting with the former unreservedly concerning the prospects of our numerous travellers then scattered over the neighbouring shores, the two ships remaining tenanted only by officers and a few invalids. Arrangements were made for the exploration of Petermann's Fiord, and, should the season prove favourable, for the examination of the ice-cap south of Bessels Bay. On the 30th of April Captain Stephenson returned to the "Discovery."

Until the latter end of May sledge parties were continually arriving or departing; carrying forward depôts of provisions for the use of the distant parties on their return.

In carrying out these duties I was much indebted to
Dr. Edward L. Moss, who again volunteered to command a
sledge ; and I the more readily availed myself of his services
knowing that it would afford him a wider field for continuing
his scientific studies.

Mr. James Wootton, Engineer, also assisted me materially
as commander of a slegde party.

On the 3rd May Lieut. Giffard returned with news from
Lieut. Pelham Aldrich up to the 25th April ; his twenty-
second day out from the ship.   He reported that all his crew
were well and cheerful; but that the soft snow was causing
very heavy and slow travelling.

Good Prospects of the Expedition.

Up to this time all had gone well with the Expedition.
The two ships had advanced as far north as was possible;
they were admirably placed for exploration and other purposes ; and the sledge crews, formed of men in full health
and strength, had obtained a fair start on their journeys
under as favourable circumstances as possible.

Outbreak of Scurvy.

On the 3rd of May Dr. Thomas Colan reported that five
men had scorbutic symptoms ; however, as each case had
some predisposing cause I was not alarmed, until on the 8th
the three ice quarter-masters and two able seamen returning from sledge service were attacked; by the 8th of June
fourteen of the crew of the " Alert " and three men belonging to the " Discovery " who happened to be on board,
forming the majority of the number of men then present,
had been or were under the doctor's care for the same wast-
ing disorder.   Captain Stephenson also reported that four
more of his crew had been attacked.

Although many of the sledge crews formerly employed on
Arctic research had been attacked by this disease, some had
totally escaped ; therefore, considering the ample equipment
and carefully prepared provisions with which the " Alert "

and " Discovery " were provided, its outbreak was most inexplicable and unlooked for. It was, however, most encouraging to learn from the report of former expeditions how transient the attacks had usually proved; and how readily the patients recovered with rest, the advance of summer, and a change to a more generous diet.

News from Greenland Division.

On the 9th of May, by the return of Lieutenant May and Mr. Egerton from Greenland, whither they had carried supplies and succeeded in discovering a practicable overland route immediately east of Cape Brevort fit for the use of the returning sledges should the ice break up, I received news of Lieutenant Beaumont's party up to the 4th May, when he was within two miles of Cape Stanton. From their place of crossing the Straits they found that the coast line for nearly the entire distance to Cape Stanton was formed either by precipitous cliffs or very steep snow slopes, the bases of which receive the direct and unchecked pressure of the northern pack as it drifts from the north-westward and strikes against that part of the coast nearly at right angles. The floe-bergs, at their maximum sizes, were pressed high up one over the other against the steep-shore; the chaos outside was something indescribable, and the travelling the worst that can possibly be imagined; seven days being occupied in moving forward only 20 miles. Being quite uncertain when such a road might become impassable by the ice breaking up in May, as it did in 1872, a depôt of provisions, sufficient for a return journey by land, was wisely left; but Lieutenant Beaumont's journey was thus shortened considerably.

As nearly every south-westerly wind we experienced at Floeberg Beach changed its direction to N.W. before it blew itself out, the coast of Greenland north of Cape Brevort must necessarily be a very wild one as regards ice pressure, and a most uncertain coast for navigation. A vessel once caught in the pack ice off that shore, if not crushed at once, runs a great risk of being carried by it to the eastward round the northern coast, as pointed out by Admiral Sir George Back, Kt., F.R.S.

During the first week in May the temperature rising to zero enabled me to remove the snow from over the skylights and bull's-eyes, and let in light between decks: but, owing to there being no skylight over the lower deck it still remained very dark. I would here remark, Sir, how very important it is that Arctic ships should, if possible, be fitted with a large skylight above the ship's company's living deck.

On the 24th of May Lieutenant Giffard returned on board, after depositing Lieutenant Pelham Aldrich's last depôt of provisions, he and his crew having performed their important work well and expeditiously; but I am sorry to add that he brought Dr. Colan two more invalids. The attack occurring on his outward journey; as it was of vital importance that he pushed on, Lieutenant Giffard was necessarily obliged to leave them in a snow hut for five days, one man taking care of the other as best he could until the party returned. Lieutenant Giffard acted with great judgment, decision, and consideration on this occasion, and the two invalids recovered before the ship broke out of winter quarters.

On the 1st of June Mr. Crawford Conybeare arrived with news from the "Discovery" up to the 22nd of May. Lieutenant Archer had completed his examination of the opening in the land west of Lady Franklin Sound; proving it to be a deep fiord terminating in mountainous land with glacier-covered valleys in the interior.

Lieutenant Reginald B. Fulford, with the men returned from Lieutenant Archer's party, then transported two boats across Hall's Basin to assist Lieutenant Beaumont in his return later in the season. Captain Stephenson, accompanied by Mr. Henry C. Hart, naturalist, overtook this party on the 12th at Polaris Bay. On the following day, the American flag being hoisted, a brass tablet prepared in England was erected at the foot of Captain Hall's grave with due solemnity. It bore the following inscription :—

Tablet at Captain Hall's Grave.

" Sacred
to the Memory of
CAPTAIN C. F. HALL,
of the U.S. Ship ' Polaris,'
who sacrificed his Life
in the advancement of Science,
on the 8th November, 1871.

" This Tablet has been erected by the British
Polar Expedition of 1875, who, following in his
footsteps, have profited by his experience."

Polaris Cairns and Boat Depôt at Newman's Bay visited.

Dr. Coppinger, when returning from assisting Lieutenant
Beaumont, had visited Captain Hall's Cairn at Cape Brevort
and the boat depôt in Newman's Bay ; and conveyed the few
articles of any value to the " Discovery." The boat itself,
with the exception of one hole easily repairable, was in a
serviceable condition.

Captain Stephenson returned to the " Discovery " on the
18th May, leaving Lieutenant Fulford and Dr. Coppinger on
the Greenland shore to explore Petermann Fiord.

Mr. Crawford Conybeare having reported that the travelling along shore in Robeson Channel was fast becoming
impracticable, in consequence of the ice being in motion
near the shore, his party were kept on board the " Alert."

Northern Division of Sledges.

On the evening of the 8th June Lieutenant A. A. C. Parr
arrived on board, most unexpectedly, with the distressing
intelligence that nearly the whole of the crew belonging to
the northern division of sledges were attacked with scurvy
and in want of immediate assistance. Commander Mark-

ham, and the few men who were able to keep on their feet,
had succeeded in conveying the invalids to the neighbourhood of Cape Joseph Henry, thirty miles distant from the
ship, but each day was rapidly adding to the intensity of the
disease, and, while lessening the powers of those still able to
work, adding to the number of the sick, and consequently
alarmingly increasing the weight which had to be dragged
on the sledges.   Under these circumstances, Lieutenant
Parr, with his usual brave determination, and knowing
exactly his own powers, nobly volunteered to bring me the
news and so obtain relief for his companions.   Starting with
only an Alpine stock and a small allowance of provisions,
he completed his long solitary walk over a very rough icy
road deeply covered with newly fallen snow within twenty-
four hours.

Arrangements were immediately made to proceed to Commander Markham's assistance; and with the help of the
officers, who at once all volunteered to drag the sledges, I
was able by midnight to proceed with two strong parties,
Messrs. Egerton, Conybeare, Wootton, and White, the
officers who could be best spared from the ship, taking their
places at the drag ropes, Lieutenant W. H. May and Dr. E.
Moss pushing on ahead with the dog-sledge laden with
appropriate medical stores.

By making a forced march the two latter, with James
Self, A.B., reached Commander Markham's camp within fifty
hours of the departure of Lieutenant Parr; although they
were, I deeply regret to state, unfortunately too late to save
the life of George Porter, Gunner, R.M.A., who only a few
hours previously had expired and been buried in the floe:
their arrival had a most exhilarating effect on the stricken
party, who were gallantly continuing their journey as best
they could.   Early on the following day I joined them with
the relief party when the hope and trust which had never
deserted these determined men was quickened to the utmost;
even the invalids losing the depression of spirits always
induced by the insidious disease that had attacked them;
and which in their case was much intensified by the recent

loss of their comrade. Early on the morning of the 14th, owing to the skill and incessant attention of Dr. E. Moss and the assistance of the dog-sledge conducted by Lieutenant May and James Self, A.B.; who, with a most praiseworthy disregard of their own rest, were constantly on the move, Commander Markham and I had the satisfaction of reaching the ship without further loss of life; and, after a general expression of thanksgiving to God for his watchful care over the lives of the survivors, of placing them under the skilful charge of Dr. T. Colan, fleet-surgeon.

Of the original seventeen members composing the party, only five—the two officers and three of the men, John Radmore, chief carpenter's mate, Thomas Jolliffe, first-class petty officer, and William Maskell, A.B.—were able to drag the sledges alongside. Three others, Edward Laurence, captain forecastle, George Winston, A.B., and Daniel Harley, captain foretop, manfully kept on their feet to the last; submitting to extreme pain and fatigue rather than by riding on the sledge increase the weight their enfeebled companions had to drag; and were just able to walk on board the ship without assistance. The remaining eight, after a long struggle, had been forced to succumb to the disease, and were carried on the sledges.

Out of the whole number the two officers alone escaped the attack of scurvy. After a few days' rest and attention, John Radmore, chief carpenter's mate, returned to his duty, and three of the others were able to attend on their sick comrades; but Thomas Jolliffe, who had most manfully resisted the disease while actively employed, when his legs became cramped from resting on his return on board, was one of the most lingering cases.

These men gradually recovered, and were all out of the sick list before the ship was free of the ice during the passage home.

Nature of Ice travelled over by Northern Division.

In journeying to the northward, the route, after leaving the coast, seldom lay over smooth ice; the somewhat level floes or fields, although standing at a mean height of 6 feet above the neighbouring ice, were small; usually less than a mile across. Their surfaces were thickly studded over with rounded blue-topped ice humps, of a mean height above the general level of from 10 to 20 feet, lying sometimes in ranges,. but more frequently separated at a distance of from 100 to 200 yards apart, the depressions between being filled with snow deeply scored into ridges by the wind; the whole composition being well comparable to a suddenly frozen oceanic sea. Separating these floes, as it were by a broadened outhedge, lay a vast collection of debris of the previous summer's broken-up pack ice, which had been re-frozen during the winter into one chaotic rugged mass of angular blocks of various heights up to 40 and 50 feet, and every possible shape, leaving little, if any, choice of a road over, through, or round about them. Among these was a continuous series of steep-sided snow drifts sloping down from the highest altitude of the pressed-up ice, until lost in the general level at a distance of about 100 yards. The prevailing wind during the previous winter having been from the westward, and the sledges' course being due north, these "sastrugi," instead of rendering the road smoother, as they frequently do in travelling along a coast line, when advantage can be taken of their long smooth tops, had to be encountered nearly at right angles. The whole formed the roughest line of way imaginable without the slightest prospect of ever improving.

The journey was consequently an incessant battle to overcome ever recurring obstacles; each hard-won success stimulating them for the next struggle. A passage-way had always to be cut through the squeezed-up ice with pickaxes, (an extra one being carried for the purpose) and an incline picked out of the perpendicular side of the high floes, or roadway built up, before the sledges, generally one at a time, could be brought on. Instead of advancing with a steady walk, the usual means of progression, more than half of each day was expended by the whole party facing the sledge and pulling it forward a few feet at a time. Under these circumstances, the distance attained, short as it may be considered by some, was truly marvellous.

The excellent conduct of the crews and the spirit displayed by them, combined with the work performed, indicated in a striking manner the sense of confidence in the leaders which they enjoyed, and points unmistakably to the watchful care taken of themselves and to the general good guidance of the party.

No two officers could have conducted this arduous journey with greater ability or courage than Commander Albert H. Markham and his very able second in command, Lieutenant A. C. Chase Parr, and I trust that their Lordships will notice their services by some mark of approval.

The services of Thomas Rawlings and Edward Laurence, 1st class petty officers, filling the highly important positions of captains of the sledges, were beyond all praise. In addition to their general cheerfulness and good humour ; to their care and skill must be attributed the safe return of the sledges, on which the lives of the party depended, uninjured and in as serviceable a state as when they left the ship ; notwithstanding the heavy nature of the road, which on all former occasions, not only repulsed the travellers altogether, but drove them back with broken-up equipment.

To such men as these, and the sledge crews generally ; it is difficult to find any reward which can in the least compensate them for the manner in which they have manfully met the extreme privations and continuous labour necessarily undergone.

Result of Attempt to journey North over the Polar Ice.

During this memorable journey to penetrate towards the north over the heavy Polar oceanic ice, without the assistance of continuous land along which to travel ; in which has been displayed in its highest state the pluck and courageous determination of the British seaman to steadily persevere, day after day, against apparently insurmountable difficulties, their spirits rising as the oppositions increased ; Commander Markham and Lieutenant Parr and their brave associates succeeded in advancing the National Flag to latitude 83° 20' 26" N., leaving a distance of 400 miles still to be travelled over before the North Pole is reached.

In order to attain this position, although a direct distance of only 73 miles from the ship was accomplished, the total distance travelled was 276 miles on the outward, and 245 miles on the homeward journey.

Their severe labour and exertions, which certainly can never be surpassed, coupled with the experience gained by Sir Edward Parry in the summer of 1827, proves that a lengthened journey over the Polar pack ice with a sledge party provided with a navigable boat is, in consequence of the rough nature of the road over which the party has to travel, impracticable at any season of the year; and further, as the sledges were necessarily advanced each stage singly, we are enabled to estimate the exact rate of progression which may be expected should any one consider it desirable to push forward with light sledges without any additional means of returning later in the season in the event of the ice breaking up in his rear. The maximum rate of advance in this way was at the rate of $2\frac{3}{4}$ miles a day, the mean being at the rate of $1\frac{1}{4}$ miles a day.

It may be necessary here to state that the much to be deplored outbreak of scurvy, which certainly shortened the journey to the extent of some 10 or 20 miles, in no way affects the conclusions to be derived from it. When the first two men who were attacked complained of sore legs, the disorder so commonly experienced by travellers in all countries, and particularly those employed to drag arctic sledges, the loss of their services at the drag ropes was fully balanced by one of the two boats being left behind; thus, the daily distance accomplished during the first 25 days of the outward journey was not materially altered, and it was only during the latter 14 days that, owing to the gradual break-down of three more of the crew, the rate of advance was necessarily much retarded. The previous rate however had been so slow that the party gallantly continued their advance to the utmost limit of their provisions; confident that, with the help of the manual labour of the officers, who from the first took their places at the drag-ropes and pickaxes and worked as hard as the men, they could readily return to the land along the road on which they had expended so much labour in somewhat levelling during their outward journey.

___

Anxiety about Western Division.

The scurvy by this time having, with very few exceptions, attacked the whole ship's company, I was somewhat anxious concerning the health of Lieutenant Aldrich's men returning from their western journey; particularly when I observed that the cairn erected over his depôt of provisions, 30 miles to the N.W., remained untouched on the day appointed for his arrival there; accordingly I sent Lieutenant May with the dog sledge and three strong men to meet him. On the 20th June the two parties joined company at the depôt and signalled their arrival to the ship. Lieutenant Aldrich had crossed the land only just in time; for on the following day a gale of wind from the southward commenced, bringing warmer weather, and the thaw set in with such rapidity that the snow valleys on the land were rendered impassable for sledges for the remainder of the season. Lieutenant May met the party on the very last day that most of them were able to travel; having succeeded in reaching, after a very severe journey, most courageously borne, the same position to which Commander Markham's party had returned without assistance: but there the same blight that attacked the northern party, and against which the western division had long been struggling, gained on them so quickly that, with the exception of Lieutenant Aldrich and Adam Ayles (P. O., 2nd cl.), the whole crew of seven men were placed *hors de combat*, James Doidge (1st cl. P.O.) and David Mitchell (A.B.) still gallantly struggling along by the side of the sledge; the other four invalids, having held out until the last moment, were obliged to be carried. Under these circumstances the arrival of Lieutenant May with relief was most providential.

With their assistance Lieutenant Aldrich succeeded in

F

reaching the "Alert" on the morning of the 26th, when, after again publicly returning thanks to the Almighty God for his watchful care over the lives of the party, they were placed under Dr. Colan's charge; the Officer being the only one not attacked by scurvy.

Notwithstanding a bad start, owing to the necessity of crossing the land with heavily laden sledges; Lieutenant Aldrich with great energy succeeded in exploring the coast line to the westward for a distance of 220 miles from the position of the "Alert." Trending first to the North Westward for 90 miles to Cape Columbia, the extreme northern cape in Lat. 83° 7′ N. and Long. 70° 30′ W., the coast extends to the West for 60 miles to Long. 79° 0′ W. and then gradually trends round to the southward, to Lat. 82° 16′ N. and Long. 85° 33′ W. the extreme position attained. No land or appearance of land was seen at any time to the northward or westward; and, owing to the continued heavy nature of the ice, I conclude that no land can possibly exist within an attainable distance from this coast.

Although most of the party suffered more or less during the outward journey, the attack was supposed to be merely transient, and it was not until they were returning home, when the scorbutic symptoms of sore gums first made their appearance, that the real nature of the disease was in the least suspected.

To these men equal praise is due as to their comrades employed in the northern division for the endurance and intrepidity with which each individual performed his respective duty. Crippled nearly as badly, they if possible suffered more severely; for being so distant from relief none could be carried without imperilling all, and each was obliged to remain toiling at the drag ropes making forced marches.

It is to Lieutenant Aldrich's judicious care and energy during the long and anxious homeward march, seconded by the spirited example of Joseph Good, acting chief boatswain's mate, captain of the sledge, himself one of the most enfeebled of the party, that they owe their lives.

Lieutenant Aldrich's services on this, as on all other

occasions during the three years he has been under my command, calls for my unqualified admiration; he is a talented and zealous officer, and in every way deserving of their Lordships' consideration.

Again, Sir, I have to bring to your notice the valuable services of Lieutenant May and James Self, A.B.; the thaw having set in, it was principally due to their incessant labour that the party arrived on board before the rapidly advancing disease had further developed itself.

Attack of Scurvy.

With regard to the outbreak of scurvy, which attacked the crew of the " Discovery " as well as ourselves ; when the sledge crews started early in April a finer body of men in apparently perfect health it would have been difficult to pick anywhere ; and I trusted that, owing to the excellent condition of our provisions, we were secure from any attack : but I must now conclude that disease was even then lurking among us, and that the heavy labour of sledge travelling intensified and brought it out, as has been the case in nearly all former journeys when the travellers have been unable to procure large supplies of game, and were unprovided with lime juice. It attacked first the weakly men, afterwards the strong men who were predisposed for it, and most severely of all those who were employed on the longest and most trying journeys.

Had there been no sledging work I believe that the disease would not have betrayed its presence amongst us, and had the officers been called upon *from the first* to perform as severe daily labour as their men I think that they would have been equally attacked.

On the 9th July, fifteen days after the return of the last sledge party, 36 of the crew of the ship had been, and 24 were, under treatment for scurvy.

This large number of patients, most of them requiring constant and special attention, necessarily taxed to the utmost the services of Dr. Thomas Colan, Fleet Surgeon, and his able second, Dr. Ed. Moss, Surgeon. Nothing could exceed their indefatigable patience and care. The deprivation of necessary rest and exercise cheerfully submitted to by Dr. Colan, upon whom the chief responsibility fell, considerably impaired his own health, following as it did so closely on his long anxious watch by the bedside of Neil Petersen.

Proceedings of Greenland Division.

In order to preserve the continuity of the narrative; I will here report the result of Lieutenant Beaumont's exploration on the Greenland coast but which I only learnt some time afterwards.

On the 6th of August, while the "Alert" was imprisoned by the ice twenty miles north of Discovery Harbour, during her passage down Robeson Channel, Lieutenant Rawson and two men arrived with letters from Captain Stephenson containing the distressing intelligence that scurvy had attacked the Greenland Division of sledges with as much severity as it had visited the travellers from the "Alert," and that Lieutenant Beaumont was then at Polaris Bay recruiting his men.

I must refer you, Sir, to Captain Stephenson's letters and to Lieutenant Lewis A. Beaumont's report for a full detail of the proceedings of this party; but I may here mention the chief points.

I have already reported their movements up to the 5th May when Dr. Coppinger left them; Lieutenant Beaumont with two sledge crews journeying to the north-eastward along the north coast of Greenland, all apparently in good health. A very few days after, James J. Hand, A.B., who had passed the winter on board of the "Alert," showed symptoms of scurvy. As soon as the nature of the disease was decided; Lieutenant Beaumont determined to send Lieutenant Rawson with three men and the invalid back to Polaris Bay and to continue the exploration with reduced numbers.

Lieutenant Wyatt Rawson parted company on his return on the 11th of May; but owing to two more of his crew breaking down leaving only himself and one man strong enough to drag the sledge; on which lay the principal sufferer, and to look after the other two, he only succeeded in reaching the depôt on the 3rd of June; James J. Hand, unhappily dying from the extreme fatigue a few hours after the arrival of the party at Polaris Bay. Out of the other men forming the sledge crew, who had all passed the winter on board the " Alert," only one of them—Elijah Rayner, Gunner, R.M.A.—escaped the insidious disease; George Bryant, 1st Class Petty Officer and Captain of the sledge, and Michael Regan, A.B., were both attacked, the former, although in a very bad state, manfully refused to the last to be carried on the sledge, knowing that his extra weight would endanger the lives of all.

I cannot praise Lieutenant Rawson's conduct on this occasion too highly: it is entirely due to his genial but firm command of his party, inspiriting as he did his crippled band, who relied with the utmost confidence on him, that they succeeded in reaching the depôt.

His return being totally unexpected, no relief was thought of, nor, indeed, were there any men to send.

On the 7th of June Lieutenant Fulford and Dr. Coppinger, with Hans and the dog-sledge, returned to Polaris Bay depôt from the exploration of Petermann Fiord; and, with the help of some fresh seal meat and the professional skill and care of Dr. Coppinger, the malady was checked and the sick men gradually regained strength.

Lieutenant Beaumont, continuing his journey, on the 21st May succeeded in reaching lat. 82° 18' N., long 50° 40' W., discovering land, apparently an island, but, owing to the nature of the ice, probably a continuation of the Greenland coast, extending to lat. 82° 54' N., long. 48° 33' W.

By this time two more of the crew showed symptoms of scurvy; and soon after the return journey was commenced the whole party were attacked: until at last Lieutenant Beaumont, Alexander Gray, ice-quartermaster captain of the sledge, and Frank Jones, stoker, were alone able to drag; the other four men having to be carried forward on the sledge in detachments, which necessitated always double and most frequently treble journeys over the rough and disheartening icy road; nevertheless, the gallant band struggled manfully onwards thankful if they made one mile a day but never losing heart; but Lieutenant Beaumont's anxiety being intense lest relief should arrive too late to save the lives of the worst cases.

Not arriving at Polaris Bay on the day expected, Lieutenant Wyatt Rawson and Dr. Richard W. Coppinger, with Hans and the dog-sledge, started on the 22nd June to look for them : the two parties providentially meeting in Newman's Bay, 20 miles from the depôt. The following day Frank Jones being unable to drag any longer, walked; leaving the three officers and Alexander Gray to drag the four invalids, the dogs carrying on the provision and equipage. On the 27th Alexander Gray was obliged to give in, and the officers had to drag the sledge by themselves, Gray and Jones hobbling along as best they could. On the 28th, being within a day's march of the depôt with the dogs, the two worst cases were sent on in charge of Dr. Coppinger, and arrived at the end of the march; but I regret to state that Charles W. Paul, A.B., who joined the expedition from the " Valorous " at Disco, at the last moment, died shortly after their arrival.

The remainder of the party, helped by Hans and the dogs, arrived at the depôt on the 1st of July and, it being impossible to cross the strait and return to the " Discovery " before the invalids were recruited, at once settled themselves down for a month's stay; those able to get about shooting game for the sufferers with such success that they obtained a daily ration of fresh meat.

It was entirely due, under Providence, to the timely assistance dispatched by Lieutenant Rawson, who, as senior officer at Polaris Bay, when there was not time to cross Hall's Basin and inform Captain Stephenson of his apprehensions, acted promptly on his own authority and went to the relief of Lieutenant Beaumont's party, that more casualties did not occur.

After such details it is scarcely necessary for me to allude to the services of Lieutenant Beaumont. The command of the Greenland sledges, entailing as it did the crossing and recrossing of Robeson Channel—which in 1872 remained in motion all the season—required even greater care and judgment than is always necessary in the leader of an Arctic sledge party. My confidence in Lieutenant Beaumont, as expressed in my original orders to him, was fully borne out by his careful conduct of the party throughout this trying and most harassing march. He is a most judicious, determined, and intelligent leader, and as such I bring his services to the notice of their Lordships.

Captain Stephenson by personal inspection having satisfied himself that the resources of the Polaris Depôt were sufficient and appropriate for the subsistence of the men detached to the Greenland shore, although naturally anxious at their non-arrival on board the "Discovery," was not alarmed for their safety.

On the 12th of July Lieut. Fulford, with two men and the dog-sledge, was dispatched across Hall's Basin to Discovery Bay, and arrived there on the third day; having found the ice in motion on the west side of the channel and experiencing much difficulty in effecting a landing.

On the receipt of the news Captain Stephenson instantly started with a relief party, carrying medical comforts, and arrived at Polaris Bay on the 19th. On the following day the ice was in motion on both sides of the channel.

On the 29th Captain Stephenson, with Lieut. Rawson, Hans, and four able men, with two invalids who could walk, started with the dingy for Discovery Bay, and after a very wet journey they landed on the west shore on the 2nd August; Lieut. Beaumont and Dr. Coppinger, with five strong men, being left for a few days longer in order to give the other two invalids further time to recruit.

The whole party ultimately re-crossed the Strait, and arrived at Discovery Bay on the 14th August; having been

absent from their ship 120 days; several of the party who
had wintered on board of the "Alert" having been absent
since the 26th of August the previous year.

Great praise is due to Dr. Richard W. Coppinger for his
skilful treatment of the disease; living as he and the party
did for from six to eight weeks in tents on an Arctic shore
without extra resources or medicines except at the last: it
is much to his credit that on their arrival on board the
"Discovery" all the patients were able to perform their ship
duties.

Hans, Esquimaux.

All speak in the highest terms of Hans, the Esquimaux,
who was untiring in his exertions with the dog-sledge, and
in procuring game—it was owing to his patient skill in
shooting seal that Dr. Coppinger was able to regulate the
diet somewhat to his satisfaction.

Petermann Fiord.

Lieutenant Reginald B. Fulford and Dr. Richard W. Coppinger cleared up all doubt about the nature of Petermann
Fiord; having reached, at a distance of nineteen miles from
the entrance, the precipitous cliff of a glacier which stretched
across the Fiord.

Result of Spring Sledging Operations.

On considering the result of the spring sledging operations,
I concluded that, owing to the absence of land trending to
the northward and the Polar pack not being navigable, no
ship could be carried north on either side of Smith's Sound
beyond the position we had already attained; and also that
from any attainable position in Smith's Sound it was impossible to advance nearer the pole by sledges.

Decide to return to England.

The only object, therefore, to be gained by the Expedition remaining in the vicinity for another season would be to extend the exploration of the shores of Grant Land to the south-westward, and Greenland to the north-eastward eastward; but as with the whole resources of the Expedition I could not hope to advance more than about 50 miles beyond the positions already attained on those coasts, and moreover, although the crew were rapidly recovering from the disease which had attacked them, they would certainly be unfit for employment on extended sledge parties next year; I decided that the Expedition should return to England as soon as the ice broke up and released the ship. It was with the very greatest regret I felt it my duty to give up the very interesting further examination of the northern coast of Greenland.

Although pools of water formed along the tidal crack in the ice early in June the thaw did not regularly set in before the last week of the month.

On the 1st of July water in the ravines commenced to run; after that date the thaw was very rapid both on shore and on the ice but no decided motion took place before the 20th.

On the 23rd, with a strong S.W. wind, the pack was driven a mile away from the shore; but, as in the autumn, no navigable channel made to seaward or along the land to the westward of Cape Sheridan.

On the 26th, a record was left in a cairn erected on shore detailing the work performed by the Expedition and of my intention to proceed to the southward.

Start for Southward.

On the 31st, after considerable labour to clear away a passage through the barrier of floe-bergs which had so well protected us during the winter; we succeeded during a strong S.W. wind, which drove the pack out to sea, in rounding Cape Rawson and entering Robeson Channel on our return voyage.

Stopped off Cape Union.

After a 10 miles run along shore, through a fairly open channel between the pack and the cliffy ice foot bordering the coast, we were stopped by a heavy floe 1½ mile in diameter nipping against the land 4 miles north of Cape Union; and there being no other protection attainable, the ship was secured in a small indentation among a group of grounded floe-bergs lining the shore off a shallow part of the coast.

The ice in the offing drifted north and south with the tides in a nearly compact mass; that near the shore alone being loose but in no way navigable.

Early in the morning of the 1st of August, the heavy floe which had stopped us the previous day commenced to move and was soon travelling to the northward with the whole strength of the tide at the rate of 1½ mile an hour; scraping along the ice foot as it advanced towards the ship in a rather alarming manner. Steam being fortunately ready we cast off, and succeeded in passing between it and the shore as, after a severe wrench against a projecting point close ahead of us, a channel was opened by its rebound; and as it coach-wheeled round the north point of the floe turned in towards the land close to the position which we had vacated a few moments before.

Comparison of Ordinary Floe and Polar Sea Ice.

The difference between an ordinary floe and Polar Sea ice was here exemplified completely; the former, composed of ice about 6 feet in thickness, on meeting with an obstruction is torn in pieces as it presses past it; the latter being some 80 or 100 feet thick, quietly lifts any impediment away out of its course and takes no further notice of it. Such was the case on this occasion: the polar floe, which we only escaped by a few yards, on nipping against the heavy breastwork of isolated floe-bergs lining the coast, some of them 40 feet high and many thousand tons in weight, which had lately formed our protection from the smaller ice pieces, tilted them over one after another and forced them higher up the land slope, like a giant at play; without receiving the slightest harm itself, not a piece breaking away. It was most providential that by its twisting round the "Alert" was enabled to escape out of the trap in which she was enclosed.

Steering onward, so close to the shore ice-cliff, from twenty to forty feet high and having ten to twenty fathoms water alongside it, that the quarter-boats touched on several occasions, we reached within two miles of Cape Union, but in consequence of the pack remaining close in at the cape, both during the flood and ebb tides, the ship was again brought to a stop. Fortunately we were able to secure her abreast of a large water course, the stream of which had been powerful enough to undermine the ice-cliff to such an extent as to allow fifty yards of it to break away and float off to sea; this left just sufficient space in which to secure the ship alongside the beach in such a manner that in the event of a nip taking place she would merely be forced on the shore before the floe itself grounded. Here we were delayed for twenty-four hours with the boats from the exposed side lowered down and moored in-shore for safety.

Unable to pass Cape Union.

At half flood, the south running tide, a narrow lead of water formed round the cape; steam was got up immediately; but owing to delay in shipping the rudder consequent on the tide running towards the bow carrying it under the ship's bottom, the ice closed in again before I could get round; it also cut us off from our friendly little haven; I was therefore obliged to secure the ship during the north-running tide in a slight indentation in the high cliffy ice-foot. Fortunately being within half a mile of Cape Union the run of the ice, as it passed to the northward round the Cape, kept at about twenty yards from the land until after it had passed our position; only the lighter ice pieces scraping their way along the ship's side.

As we would be exposed to the whole pressure of the ice during the south-going tide; at 4 P.M., low water, it being calm and no prospect of a westerly wind to open a navigable passage, I cast off and bored a short distance into the pack with the purpose of allowing the ship to drift round the cape with the flood or south-going tide. The ice carried her with it about a quarter of a mile distant from the land, with no navigable water in sight, the whole pack moving steadily together without nipping to any great extent. As we passed we noticed that the front of the ice-foot was perfectly smooth and would afford no protection whatever if we were obliged to leave the pack.

As the tide slackened we succeeded with great trouble in steaming out of the pack just as the ice commenced to set to the northward with great rapidity. As it remained slack for some 20 yards from the beach, we were able to proceed steaming slowly to the southward close to the ice foot; the midship boats being turned in-board, but the quarter boats which could not be protected, being in constant peril of a squeeze against the cliffy ice wall bordering the shore. The water channel widening considerably as we approached Lincoln Bay; we crossed it without any trouble, and arrived within 5 miles of Cape Beechy before the tide turned to run south again; when I secured the ship alongside a heavy polar floe-piece, with the hope of again drifting south, but finding that the lighter pieces of ice were drifting faster and gradually enclosing us, I was obliged to cast off; and with much trouble succeeded in reaching the north side of Cape Beechy, before the north-running tide made at noon, August 3rd.

Stopped by the Ice South of Cape Beechy.

After two hours' waiting, there being plenty of water space to the northward, a channel opened and allowed us to get round the Cape. Here the cliffy ice-foot comes to an end with the precipitous land. South of the Cape the land slopes down to the shore line, and is fronted by a breastwork of broken-off floe-bergs similar to, but somewhat smaller than, those lining the shore of the Polar Sea; among these the ship was secured in three fathoms water within twenty yards of the shore, a mile south of the Cape, and considering our much more exposed position during the winter, I thought the ship secure.

During the 4th of August the weather was overcast with snow squalls from the S.W., with a low barometer but not much wind. As the ice had closed in and locked the ship up completely, the sportsmen visited the lakes where three musk-oxen had been shot the previous summer. A number of geese were found all unable to fly, the old ones moulting were nearly featherless, and the young ones although well grown were yet unfledged; consequently fifty-seven were captured : a very welcome supply for the invalids, of whom we had ten still remaining.

Communication with " Discovery."

The ice remaining close, and being only twenty miles from the "Discovery," Mr. Egerton, with a seaman for a companion, was sent to her on the 5th of August, with orders for her to prepare for sea. They had a rough and troublesome walk over the hills but arrived the same evening.

Pack in the Offing.

During our detention at this position the pack in the offing drifted up and down the strait with the tide, the wind having the effect of increasing the speed of the current and the duration of its flow both towards the north and the south. Although the ice generally was of a considerably lighter character than that in the Polar Sea, or at the northern entrance of Robeson Channel; a number of heavy polar floes passed us, driven to the southward by the northerly wind; and set into Lady Franklin Sound and Archer Fiord rather than down Kennedy Channel. In fact, that sound may be considered as a pocket receiving all the heavy ice driven southward through Robeson Channel, and retaining it until the prevailing westerly winds carry it to the northward again and clear out the Sound ready to be re-filled when the north wind returns. It is only during seasons when northerly winds prevail considerably over the westerly ones that the heavy polar ice is carried south in large quantities into Smith's Sound and Baffin's Bay.

Pressure of the Pack against stranded Floe-bergs.

On the 6th of August the wind increased considerably from the north until it blew a gale. During the height of the flood or south-going tide a succession of heavy floe pieces passed us drifting down the strait; toying with our barrier of outlying protectors, and turning one large one completely topsy-turvy. It was firmly aground in 12 fathoms water on an off-lying shoal some 200 yards from the main line of the floe-bergs, and on this and the previous day had been of great service in keeping the line of the drifting pack at a safe distance from us; but on this occasion the point of a large floe which was drifting south close in-shore brought the weight of the whole pack on the doomed mass; as it received the pressure the floe-berg was reared up in the air to its full height of at least 60 feet above water, and turning a complete somersault fell over on its back with a tremendous splash, breaking into a number of pieces with a great commotion and raising a wave sufficient to roll the ship considerably.

Ship nipped.

Our protecting floe-berg carried away, the ice moved in forcing the lighter floe-bergs one after the other, as they became exposed, farther in-shore, and at last nipped the ship slightly.

This evening Lieutenant Rawson and two seamen arrived from the "Discovery" with news of the Greenland division of sledges.

On the morning of the 7th of August, with the wind blowing slightly off the land, the ice eased off shore and cleared the nip round the ship, but did not allow me to move to a more sheltered position.

In the afternoon, a temporary opening occurring, steam was raised and the rudder shipped but, owing to some of the ropes fouling, the latter was not ready before the ice closed in and imprisoned us again.

During the night the wind increased considerably and with the south running tide the ice was being carried past us at the rate of 2 miles an hour.

Owing to several heavy pieces grounding outside our line of barrier ice, the inner edge of the pack was guided more towards our position; and at last two heavy pieces wedged themselves against the ship, the inner one grounding alongside the ship after forcing her very close to the shore, and nipping her to such an extent that the ship was raised bodily 3 feet. As the tide rose the lighter ice in-shore gradually forced its way under the ship's bottom and relieved the pressure somewhat; so that after four hours she was only raised about 6 inches above her usual draught of water.

Arrive at Discovery Bay.

As there was now no hope of releasing the ship, except by cutting down the heavy piece of ice which was aground outside us, all hands were set to work with pickaxes to lighten it. On the 10th of August, after three days' work, the ice having been sufficiently reduced, floated at the top of high water and the ship was freed; the main pack moving off shore at the same time, we advanced five miles, and on the following day, after much trouble, succeeded in joining company with the " Discovery."

Sending all my sick men to the " Discovery," the " Alert " was secured at the entrance of the harbour ready to start for Polaris Bay to relieve Lieutenant Beaumont immediately the ice permitted me to cross; but his arrival on the 14th of August, as before stated, fortunately rendered this passage unnecessary.

The " Discovery " having embarked her coals and provisions, both ships were now ready to continue their voyage to the southward; but although water was observed in Kennedy

Channel the whole of Lady Franklin Sound remained filled with the ice brought to the southward by the late northerly gale.

While waiting, ready to start, each of the ships tailed on shore at nearly low water but floated again without damage.

Cross Lady Franklin Sound.

We were delayed here with calm weather and consequent little motion in the ice until the 20th of August; when, a chance offering, we pushed our way through the pack, which gradually opening as we advanced, led us into comparatively open water off Cape Lieber ; where a strong south-westerly wind which had not been able to force its way across the ice in Hall's Basin had been blowing for several days.

As we neared Cape Laurence, the ice, which had been getting closer as we advanced south, became so close that we must either return north, run into the pack, or secure the ships to some of the grounded floebergs or icebergs. I chose the latter course, and entering the bay immediately south of the cape, we followed the coast until we found ourselves in a large inner basin perfectly land-locked ; and I made the ships fast with perfect confidence although with the spring flood-tide the ice was floating sluggishly in and gradually filling up the bay.

"Alert" pressed on Shore.

It happened, unfortunately, that at the very top of high-water a rather insignificant-looking piece of ice pressed against the ship when the floe-berg in-shore of us, and against which the ship was resting, had floated with the spring tide and allowed itself to be pressed in-shore ; suddenly we found the ship aground forward with deep water under the stern.

Before any means could be taken to release her from this position she was helplessly fixed. At low water the tide had fallen fourteen feet, leaving the fore foot and keel bare as far aft as the fore channels ; the ship lying over on her bilge at an angle of twenty-two degrees.

As the tide rose the ship was lightened, the cables hauled aft, and the anchors lowered on to suitable pieces of ice. One of these was then hauled astern to a proper position when by blowing up the ice the anchor was laid out with great ease. At high water the ship was hauled off without having received any injury.

On the 22nd of August a S.W. wind opened a passage again; of which immediate advantage was taken, and we proceeded to the southward as far as Cape Collinson with only the ordinary troubles in ice navigation during thick snow storms, misty weather, and strong head winds.

Off the Cape, owing to "Alert" being obliged to back astern to escape a nip, the two ships fouled for a few moments, and the "Discovery" lost a boat's davit, but by smart and skilful management saved the boat.

I may here add that such has been the skill displayed by the officers of the watches of the "Alert" and "Discovery," although the two ships have frequently been necessarily within touching distance of each other, and of the ice cliffs and bergs, this is the only accident of consequence which occurred during the voyage.

The ice closing in ahead; the two ships were made fast inside some grounded icebergs in Joiner Bay one mile north of Cape McClintock.

Northern Limit of Icebergs on West Side of Channel.

In Rawlings Bay, south of Cape Laurence, icebergs are found for the first time in numbers on coming from the northward. All to the northward may be considered as floe-bergs. Few even of the initiated can distinguish one from the other so like are they; certainly any stranger would be deceived the floe-bergs being frequently larger than the icebergs.

The ice-foot is also totally different; being formed by the pressure of lighter ice. it does not project into such deep water: consequently, whereas we could secure the ship along-side the ice-foot in Robeson Channel with confidence of her

G

not grounding, in Kennedy Channel and all parts to the south of it there is only one fathom water alongside the icy cliff at low water.

Starting again in the evening; as an increasing S.W. wind gradually opened the ice to the southward, we crossed Scoresby Bay; which, extending from fifteen to twenty miles in a S.W. direction, was perfectly clear of ice; the fresh breeze blowing down it raising a sea which caused the ships to pitch slightly and materially stopped their speed through the water.

Approaching Cape Frazer the wind was blowing a whole gale; and I was forced to expend much coal in reaching Maury Bay immediately north of it: in which the two ships were anchored among a lot of grounded ice but the squalls off the land rendered it anything but a safe or comfortable position.

Round Cape Frazer.

We were delayed three days rounding Cape Frazer and Cape Hayes; the turning point of the channel and consequently a troublesome piece of navigation.

On the 25th, after twice being driven back into Maury Bay, we succeeded in securing the ships inside some grounded icebergs near Cape Louis Napoleon; the same in all probability that sheltered us when bound to the northward the previous spring.

Much has been said concerning the expected difficulty of passing Cape Frazer, on account of the two flood tides, one coming south from the Polar Sea, and the other north from the Atlantic, being supposed to meet there, and by so doing collect a quantity of ice in the neighbourhood. Were ice navigation dependent on tidal currents alone; then, at the position of slack water, where there is a minimum ebb and flow, a vast quantity of ice might be collected by the two flood tides; but on the other hand there would be an equal chance of the two tides carrying it away in opposite directions: however, as wind is of far greater importance than tidal movement the case need not be considered.

Polar Sea and Atlantic Tide meeting at Cape Frazer.

The two tides do meet at Cape Frazer; the actual position varying a few miles north or south according to the prevailing wind : and, also, the ice is certainly accumulated immediately about and south of the Cape in great abundance. But this is owing to the ending of Kennedy Channel; and the strait widening considerably at that place into Smith's Sound proper. While many causes tend to keep narrow channels clear, enlarged seas with narrow outlets are naturally encumbered with ice.

I found no greater danger or trouble in passing Cape Frazer than in navigating elsewhere, except from what is caused by that cape being the turning point of the coast line; where no one wind blowing up or down the strait is able to clear away the ice on the north and south sides of the cape at the same time.

Struggling slowly and patiently along gaining about one mile a day, by moving forward from the protection of one stranded iceberg to that of another, as slight movements in the ice during the calm weather allowed; and, although obliged to enter the pack occasionally, always keeping as near the shore as prudent, we rounded Cape Louis Napoleon and on the 29th arrived at Prince Imperial Island, in Dobbin Bay: every one heartily thankful to be out of the pack, clear of the straggling icebergs, and for the ships to be secured to fixed ice once more.

During the previous week we had experienced much misty weather with a heavy fall of snow, measuring five inches; which changed the whole aspect of the land by re-clothing the richly-tinted stratified mountains with their winter garb, from which they had only been free for a short seven weeks : afterwards the snow only melted slightly in the low-lying valleys.

A northerly wind now set in; not strong enough to effect the movements of the ice materially but sufficiently so to clear the atmosphere and lower the temperature considerably below freezing-point; after this date the young sea ice formed continually day and night.

As the mist cleared away it disclosed a fine panorama of lofty snow-clad mountains with glacier-filled valleys intervening. One large one extending to the shore discharges numerous icebergs into Dobbin Bay.

Empress Eugénie Glacier.

This, the largest discharging glacier on the west shore of Smith Sound, was named after the Empress Eugénie; who, besides taking a personal interest in the expedition by her thoughtful present of a number of homely but most useful articles, added considerably to the comfort and amusement of each individual.

Cross Dobbin Bay.

On the 1st September we crossed Dobbin Bay, and succeeded in securing the ships to an iceberg aground only a quarter of a mile from the depôt of provisions left by us the previous Spring a few miles north of Cape Hawkes; but such was the thickness of the newly formed ice that boat work was nearly out of the question: by working as the cracks opened by the ebb tide some of the provisions were embarked; but there is still a boat and a large quantity of biscuit left on shore there.

The same reason prevented my landing on Washington Irving Island and visiting our own cairn until the third day; when, the Spring tide having opened a water passage, I found that our notice had not been visited since we left it.

Cairns on Washington Irving Island.

The two old cairns erected by a former traveller were again visited; the lichens which had spread from stone to stone proving that they are undoubtedly of very ancient date.

They were probably erected to mark the farthest north point reached by one of our enterprising and gallant predecessors who never returned home.

On the 3rd of September a lane of water opening along shore to the westward of Cape Hawkes every exertion was made to reach it; but, owing to the newly made ice, which by cementing together a number of loose pieces of old ice formed a barrier between us and the water, we only succeeded after long perseverance in ramming our way through it at a large expenditure of coal. After rounding the Cape; the pack by drifting away from the land had left unfrozen water and numerous detached small floes which forced us to make a very serpentine course and occasionally to pass within thirty yards of the low ice-foot on the shore; fortunately always finding deep water.

The outer pack, consisting of heavy ice, was closely cemented together by this year's frost; it contained fewer icebergs than we observed last year.

We succeeded in reaching Allman Bay, halfway between Cape Hawkes and Franklin Pierce Bay, but here the water ended, and the new ice was so strong that I thought it better to wait for the chance of an opening instead of forcing our way through it with full steam. On the following day, no sign of an opening occurring and wishing to get to a more sheltered position on the western side of the bay; the " Discovery " being better adapted for the work than the " Alert," led the way under full steam forcing a canal through the ice, which was 1 to 3 inches thick. She was several times completely stopped; until with all hands running from side to side on the upper deck and rolling the ship, she cleared herself and obtained headway again.

At the head of Allman Bay we found a long valley, leading down from the lofty hills far back in the interior, filled with a gigantic glacier, probably extending eastward nearly to Dobbin Bay. It was named after Mr. Evans, the President of the Geological Society.

Water under Glaciers when the Temperature of Air is below Freezing Point.

In the Bay the temperature of the surface water was 32 degrees; whereas since the frost had set in we had not met with any above 30 degrees. On testing it was found to be nearly fresh which fully accounted for the increased thickness of the newly formed ice. We afterwards found the same phenomenon in the neighbourhood of each glacier stream that we passed: proving that the water under the glaciers, being cut off from the increasing cold, remains unfrozen and running after the temperature of the air is considerably below freezing point.

The ice prevented our further movement until the 6th September. Early on the 7th, after one halt to allow the ice to open, we reached Norman Lockyer Island, finding water channels for a third of the way across Princess Marie Bay. The season was now getting so late that one false step would probably entail our passing another winter in these seas without any adequate result being derived; therefore before attempting to cross the bay, I walked to the summit of the island with Captain Stephenson; and from there we had the cheering prospect of seeing a large space of open water some twenty miles distant from us, which we knew would extend to the entrance of Smith's Sound, with only a few troublesome looking nips between us and it. Making a signal to to the ships, we hurried on board, and with the exception of one nip, which cost us an hour to clear away with all hands on the ice and the " Discovery " charging at it repeatedly with full steam, we succeeded in getting two-thirds of the distance across the Bay; but there we were stopped by three extensive Paleocrystic floes which, toggled in between some grounded bergs and Cape Victoria, prevented the ice from drifting out of Princess Marie Bay. The open water was now in sight from the mast-head, but the supply of coal was getting so low that if we did not succeed in releasing the ships the allowance for the second winter would have to be much reduced.

On the 9th, as the ice moved at the change of tides, we advanced about a mile.

On the morning of the 10th, observing that the heavy ice was likely to drift clear of the icebergs which imprisoned it, steam was got up ready; and five minutes after the channel was opened we passed through and found ourselves clear of Cape Victoria.

Charging the Last Barrier.

After this there was only one serious obstacle to our advance : owing to the very calm weather the new ice had now frozen so strong that full steam was always necessary, particularly so wherever we had to force our way through ice where scattered pieces of old ice had been re-frozen closely together. At our last barrier of this kind, after the " Alert " had repeatedly charged the nip with full steam and considerable speed on, with no result, the " Discovery" ranged up alongside, and there being a narrow piece of heavy ice which would prevent the two ships actually touching, we made a charge together and succeeded in forcing the barrier and gaining the open water beyond.

Open Water.

From here the water channel permitted me to make a clear run for Cape Sabine; the ice opening as we advanced until none was in sight from the mast head.

On passing the entrance of Hayes Sound a considerable quantity of ice was observed some distance inside it.

The Navigation of Kennedy and Robeson Channels.

In comparing the voyage of the " Polaris " and that of the " Alert " and " Discovery," I believe that a vessel might have passed up the channel with equal fortune as the " Polaris " without encountering ice during the S.W. gale we experienced in the middle of September, 1875. The heavy sea which on that occasion was produced in Robeson Channel indicated that there was a considerable stretch of clear water to the southward. The difficulty would be the choice of a starting point so late in the season after the frost has set in. If carefully navigated, a vessel, although kept ready to make a start, ought by that time to be secured in a sheltered position fit for winter quarters; and, therefore, would most probably be unable to reach the channel of opened water when it formed. If incautious, she would be as helpless in the pack. The best starting points are Port Foulke and Port Payer, at the entrance of Smith's Sound.

The "Polaris'" quick passage north was entirely due to her leaving the entrance of Smith Sound at an opportune moment late in the season; had she left at any other time she would have experienced the same trouble in getting north in 1871 as in returning south the following year. There was as much ice in the channel in 1871 as in 1872—75—76.

To the latitude of Polaris or Discovery Bay, if no accident happens to the ship, the passage may probably be made with perseverance most years, by starting early in the season : but it will at all times be a most dangerous one.

In Robeson Channel the difficulties are greatly increased, and the passage may be said to depend as much on a fortunate combination of circumstances as on skilful navigation. The present expedition was 25 days in going and the same in returning between Cape Sabine and Discovery Bay, the distance being 250 miles; 7 days in proceeding from Discovery Bay to the Arctic Sea, and 12 days in returning, the distance being 76 miles.

Sail was only used once on the passage north, the distance run being 20 miles; it was never used during the passage south. It is, therefore, totally out of the question, a sailing vessel ever making the voyage; nevertheless, as full steam was only necessary on two occasions, a powerful steamer is not necessary. When the ice is decidedly closing no power at present available is of the slightest use, when it is opening, easy speed generally carries the ship along as fast as the ice clears away in advance of her; it is rarely that a quick dash forward is necessary.

In a very exceptional season a ship might be carried nearer towards Cape Joseph Henry than Floeberg Beach on the west shore; and probably into Newman Bay on the east shore of the entrance to Robeson Channel; but from the experiences we have gained, I most confidently report that no vessel will ever round the promontory of Cape Joseph Henry or pass beyond Cape Brevoort in navigable water.

Mild Seasons in Baffin's Bay.

Every observation indicates that the last few years have been mild at the settlements on the west coast of Greenland, and open seasons with regard to the ice in Baffin's Bay; little or none having been met with north of Cape York in July and August. The settlement at the Whale Fish Islands has been temporarily withdrawn owing to the thin state of the ice rendering the fishing dangerous; and the temperature of the water as we proceeded south through Baffin's Bay was so high, that navigation can scarcely be interrupted off Disco before the end of the year; indeed the Inspector intended to be absent in an open boat in the month of November.

With a maximum body of water the ice formed on it in one winter will be considerably lighter or thinner than it would be had a quantity of ice been left floating about on its surface ready to be re-frozen thicker, and cemented with the new ice into one floe, during the coming winter. Thus, one open season certainly leads to another; and unless for-tuitous circumstances occur, such as continuous S.W. gales during the summer months, the season of 1877 must be a very open one in Baffin's Bay.

North of Smith's Sound the season is probably entirely different to that of Baffin's Bay; for the same northerly wind which carries the ice to the southward towards Davis Straits must fill up Smith's Sound with heavy polar ice and produce a cold season. Southerly winds, which keep the ice

north in the Bay, would as certainly clear out the channels
to the northward, empty the ice into the Polar Sea, and
produce a milder season than usual.

Esquimaux Migration.

From Hayes Sound northward to Cape Beechy, in latitude
81ʹ 52ʹ N., where Robeson Channel is only 13 miles across,
numerous Esquimaux remains stud the whole line of the
the west shore of Smith's Sound.   To the southward of
Cape Beechy the coast-line affords fair travelling, to the
northward the precipitous cliffs cut off all further advance
except during the depth of winter, when the ice in the
channel is stationary.   A very careful examination was made
of the coast north of Cape Union, and I can report with
confidence that Esquimaux have never had a permanent
settlement on that shore.

All the facts collected by our numerous observers lead me
to conclude that the wanderers crossed Robeson Channel
from Cape Beechy to Cape Lupton, where the Polaris Expedition discovered their traces.

Drift Wood, Evidence of the Rising of the Land.

The few pieces of drift wood, all of the fir or pine species,
that have been obtained on the shores of the Polar Sea have
evidently drifted to the position in which they were found
from the westward.   One piece was obtained lying on the
surface of the Polar Sea ice itself, two miles distant from the
land, the rest were found on the shore at different heights
above the sea-level up to 150 feet ; the former piece was
perfectly fresh with the bark on ; the latter in all stages of
decay, usually imbedded in the mud of. dry ancient lakes
evidently formed by the rising of the land, and of very great
age.

Besides these evidences of the rising of the land, the
clearly defined smoothing of the rocks at all the prominent
capes, from the present ice-level up to 300 and 400 feet until
the marks are lost in the gradually decomposing rocks,

caused by the pressure of the bordering ice-foot and the grounding ice as it is forced against the land by the drifting pack; and the numerous sea-shell beds and mud deposits at high elevations, were most noticeable.

Thickness of Ice in Winter.

At Floeberg Beach the salt-water ice formed during the winter attained its maximum thickness of 75½ inches early in June. In a fresh-water lake at the same date the ice was 79½ inches thick, with 12 feet depth of water at a temperature of 32° below it. This proves decidedly that the deep lakes do not freeze to the bottom during the winter.

Temperature of the Earth.

The lowest temperature registered by a thermometer buried 2 feet in the ground beyond the influence of any sudden variation was 13 degrees below zero; 59 degrees warmer than the air at the time. It rose gradually as the summer advanced, and at the end of July had risen to + 29·5°. By that time the ravines had nearly stopped running, and the weather was becoming gradually colder.

The sun's rays were most powerful on the 13th and 21st June, when a thermometer, with the blackened bulb in vacuo, registered + 128 and + 129 degrees, the temperature of the earth's surface at the time being + 27 and of the air + 34 degrees.

Temperature of the Sea.

The coldest temperature of the sea water during the winter was 28·25°, the same at all depths.

On several occasions NEGRETTI & ZAMBRA's REVERSIBLE THERMOMETER showed that the temperature of the surface water, south of Robeson Channel, was colder than that of the underlying stratum; the difference amounting on one occasion to 1½ degree Fahrenheit.

Tides.

At Floeberg Beach the time of high water full and change, 10h. 44m.; spring rise, 3ft. 0in.; neap rise, 1ft. 7¾in.; neap range, 0ft. 5in.

Pass Cape Sabine.

As I had deposited a notice of our proceedings at Norman Lockyer Island, and intended calling at Cape Isabella, I ran past our station near Cape Sabine without visiting it; observing that the cairn was intact, and appeared to be in the same state as we left it.

Payer Harbour and the neighbourhood was clear of ice.

We arrived off Cape Isabella on the 9th September, the weather still remaining calm. On landing, a small mail of letters and newspapers which had been left by the "Pandora" was found at the depôt, the dates informing us that the visit was made this year, but, beyond a notice stating that if possible a duplicate box of newspapers would be landed at Cape Sabine, we found no record of her previous or intended movements. Concluding that the remainder of our mail was left at Disco, and being short of coal and the weather very calm, I pushed on towards the Carey Islands; without losing time by visiting Littleton Island on the opposite side of the strait.

A southerly wind springing up, the ships were put under sail. Beating to the southward we fetched into Whale Sound on the 11th without meeting any ice since leaving Smith's Sound. The wind having freshened into a gale, I anchored in Bardin Bay on the evening of the 12th, where we observed some Esquimaux on shore; but the weather continuing very bad, I, unfortunately for them, put off communicating until the following day. On the same night the wind shifted suddenly and forced us to get under weigh; when the misty weather and a dark night prevented my landing at their settlement.

The rock a-wash off Cape Powlet, the east point of the entrance, on which the Esquimaux village stands, is very dangerous. There is no good anchorge obtainable outside of Tyndall Glacier; we were obliged to anchor in 23 fathoms in a position exposed to the northward, the "Discovery" making fast astern of the "Alert."

Unable to fetch the Carey Islands.

During the 13th and 14th we worked to the southward towards Wolstenholm Island, with calms and light airs from the west, which prevented my reaching the Carey Islands except at a large expenditure of our rapidly diminishing stock of coal; the heavy swell left from the late southerly gale would also have prevented our landing; accordingly our letters, left there the previous year by the "Pandora," were obliged to be sacrificed.

Cross to Entrance of Lancaster Sound.

From Wolstenholm Sound a south-easterly wind enabled us to fetch across to Cape Byam Martin, at the entrance of Lancaster Sound, where we arrived on the 16th; having seen no field ice and the temperature of the sea-water ranging from 31 to 34 degrees. Steaming to the eastward on the 18th, we met another S.E. wind which carried us into the south part of Melville Bay, and we proceeded south along the Greenland shore. I preferred re-crossing Baffin's Bay rather than, by standing to the southward on the west side, risk getting in-shore of the middle ice.

Arrive at Disco.

On the 20th Cape Shackleton was sighted, and on the 25th we arrived at Disco, having had persistent head winds since we left the entrance of Smith's Sound on the 10th. Only one light stream of ice was fallen in with all this part of the voyage.

Here Mr. Krarup Smith, Inspector of North Greenland, most considerately allowed us to take 30 tons of coal out of his small store, and informed me that there were 20 tons more at my disposal if I would visit Egedesminde. In order to give the Expedition the full benefit of his presence in obtaining supplies, Mr. Krarup Smith accompanied the ship to that port. Nothing could exceed his kindness to us during our stay.

Finding that several of the inhabitants of Egedesminde were attacked with scurvy, I made the Governor a present of lime-juice for general use.

From Mr. Smith we learnt that all our letters, with the exception of the few left at Cape Isabella, had been deposited at Littleton Island. Only a few letters were received at Cape Isabella; therefore a large mail of private and official correspondence has been lost.

After coaling and preparing the ships for sea, we left Egedesminde on the 2nd of October.

Passage Home.

On the 4th of October the two ships re-crossed the Arctic Circle, exactly fifteen months from the time of crossing it on the outward voyage.

Experiencing contrary winds, slow progress was made to the southward.

As the weather became warmer and damper, a few men were attacked with rheumatism and colds.

On the 12th, during a very severe gale, in which the ships were hove to under a close reefed main topsail and storm staysail, the "Alert's" rudder-head, sprung when the ship was in the ice, worked adrift from the irons with which it had been repaired; the lower part of the rudder remaining sound. As I had neglected to have the rudder pendants shackled on before leaving port it was with no little difficulty that make-shift rudder pendants were improvised; but by their means the ship has been steered across the Atlantic; the sails being trimmed to bring as little strain as possible on the rudder.

The "Discovery" was lost sight of during a heavy gale on the 19th. During the passage southerly winds prevailed.

The spare rudder, itself badly sprung, has been repaired, and is in serviceable condition; when it is shifted the

" Alert " will be ready to proceed to Portsmouth.   Captain Stephenson, before parting company, was ordered to rendez-vous at Queenstown.

Services of Officers and Ships' Companies.

In conclusion, it is my pleasing duty to inform you for the information of their Lordships, that one and all under my command have done their duty well and nobly; the utmost cordiality prevailing throughout the members of the Expedition from first to last.

Captain Stephenson has been a most valuable colleague; and I am much indebted to him for his friendly advice and ready help on all occasions.

The executive officers have each been mentioned in the detail reports of Captain Stephenson and myself; their con-duct, when taxed to the utmost under difficult and most dis-tressing circumstances, is beyond all praise.

Much as the attack of scurvy which visited us is to be regretted, it proved how valuable were the services of Fleet Surgeon Thomas Colan, M.D., and Staff Surgeon Belgrave Ninnis, M.D., who were so ably assisted by Surgeons Edward Lawton Moss, M.D., and Richard William Coppinger, M.D. These officers are each of great talent and high character; and have fully borne out the confidence imposed in them by the Medical Director-General; any reward that it is in the power of their Lordships to bestow on these gentlemen could not be given to more careful or zealous officers.

Lieutenants Lewis Anthony Beaumont and William Henry May who voluntarily undertook the navigating duties in their respective ships, have performed that work most ably.

Lieutenants May and Robert Hugh Archer have charted the coast-line from the entrance of Smith's Sound to the northward with great exactness; these officers have earned their Lordships' commendation.

The Expedition is much indebted to Mr. Thomas Mitchell, Assistant Paymaster-in-charge; the departure of the Assist-ant Paymaster of the " Alert " has much increased his work

as the only officer of his rank in the Expedition. In order
the more readily to assist me, he performed a sledge journey
in the early season from the "Discovery" to the "Alert,"
and has since then divided his time between the two ships.
He is a steady and trustworthy officer, and as such I recommend him for promotion. Mr. Mitchell and Mr. George
White, Engineer, have made a most valuable collection of
photographs of subjects connected with arctic life and scenes.

The Engineers of the two ships have always most zealously
assisted, like every one else, in the general work; and fully
occupied their spare time for the benefit of the Expedition.

Messrs. James Wootton and Daniel Cartmel deserve great
praise for the invariable excellent order in which the engines
under their charge have been kept; and for the careful
economy of the coal supply, a vital point in arctic exploration. Messrs. George White and Matthew Richard Miller
are each careful and talented officers. I most confidently
recommend the claims of these four gentlemen, who were
voluntarily employed with the support sledges, to the favourable consideration of their Lordships.

The two ships' companies have conducted themselves in
the most praiseworthy manner throughout, they are specially
commendable for their resolute perseverance during the
trying sledge journeys which have been already reported.
Their good conduct and zeal entitle them to the most
favourable consideration of their Lordships. A list of men
specially deserving of and fit for advancement to higher
rates will shortly be forwarded.

I have the honor to be,

Sir,

Your obedient Servant,

G. S. NARES, *Captain,*

Commanding Arctic Expedition.

The Secretary of Admiralty,
London.

LONDON : PRINTED BY W. CLOWES AND SONS STAMFORD STREET AND CHARING CROSS.